The
Unprejudiced
Palate

The Unprejudiced Palate

Angelo Pellegrini

LYONS & BURFORD, PUBLISHERS

Lyons & Burford, 31 West 21 Street, New York, NY 10010.
Printed in the United States of America
10 9 8 7 6 5 4 3 2 1
Library of Congress Cataloging-in-Publication Data
Pellegrini, Angelo M.
The unprejudiced palate : Angelo Pellegrini.
p.   cm.
Originally published: San Francisco : North Point Press, 1984.
ISBN 1-55821-199-3
1. Gastronomy.   2. Cookery.   I. Title.
[TX633.P38   1992]
641'.01'3—dc20
92-17250
CIP

To Virginia

*Who graciously stepped aside
that a myth might be perpetuated*

Contents

The
Unprejudiced
Palate

PART ONE

Bread and Wine
in Perspective

I

A Slight Touch
of Heresy

WE HAD just won the game that gave us the Coast Conference championship in football. Bill's parents had left that morning to spend the week end at their cottage on Puget Sound, and we were to have the house to ourselves. What an opportunity to stage a jolly undergraduate brawl! Would I prepare the dinner?

Why not? Had I any experience in cooking? No. Would I know how to proceed? Why, of course. All Italians can sing. All Italians can cook. All Italians can . . .

Bill was amazed at my confidence—and somewhat worried for we had invited, among others, a favorite professor of philosophy who was a practicing gourmet and of whom we were in considerable awe.

I had not, until then, undertaken anything more ambitious than frying an egg. And yet, I must confess my confidence was genuine. Without hesitation I proceeded with the shopping. My selection of a rabbit—mildly shocking to Bill and the girls—was an almost instinctive choice. At home, that animal had been more or less traditional fare for the Sunday dinner. Except for the artichokes, which occasioned some bewilderment, the other items on the menu were less uncommon and therefore more reassuring to my friends.

3

I said I had had no experience in cooking. Well, that is only a partial truth; for I had always lived in a delightfully culinary atmosphere and had served, so to speak, an unconscious apprenticeship in the kitchen. How often had I dressed a rabbit, or assisted Father with the task, on Saturday afternoon! How often had I gone to the garden, at Mother's bidding, to get a sprig of thyme, a bit of rosemary, a little parsley, as she salted and peppered the rabbit and laved it in olive oil preparatory to roasting it! And ho! the number of times I had minced herbs under Mother's occasionally impatient scrutiny!

Without actually being aware of it I had absorbed considerable culinary skill—had become something of a cook before I had attempted to cook anything at all. As I prepared the rabbit for the roaster, I remembered without effort a procedure that I must have unwittingly observed a thousand times. I rubbed the rabbit with garlic, salted and peppered it thoroughly, and stuffed the visceral cavity with a variety of herbs taken from the garden of an Italian acquaintance. I asked Bill for some olive oil—without success. But I had seen the article for sale in drug stores, so I asked to see the medicine cabinet. There it was, flanked by iodine and listerine! Bill told me his mother rubbed it on her scalp. He wasn't quite sure.

I poured it into the roaster and on the rabbit. While the little animal was sizzling in the oven, I cleaned and halved the artichokes, a task I had reluctantly performed hundreds of times. I minced a little garlic and parsley which I worked into the artichokes after they had blanched for a few minutes. At the proper time I put them in the pan with the rabbit and basted them carefully with the oil, which by that time had been enriched with the meat juice.

Frankly, I do not remember whether the result

even approached Mother's roast rabbit. The occasion was extraordinarily gay, thanks to an excellent wine provided by an Italian friend. The procedure and menu were sufficiently unorthodox to disarm bright western undergraduates who were hell-bent on emancipation from all traces of provincialism. I also remember having pitched their expectations rather high with the announcement that the dish had been a favorite of the sumptuous Borgias, and that all Florentines—including myself—prepare it with enviable skill. (I have learned since that even a pretty fair gourmet can be conditioned to make the proper response.)

Well! the food must have been rather good than bad. The professor was eloquent in his expressions of praise and quite metaphysical in his analysis of the flavor. He used such words as "essence," "synthesis," "substance"; and unless my memory fails me, at one point in his verbal exuberance he used the word "universal" in referring to the rabbit. To an immigrant boy who was just learning his way around at the University, the professor's performance was very impressive. What a pity that I had eaten roast rabbit so many times without enjoying its metaphysical subtleties! When dinner was over I was certain of one thing: the *particular* rabbit that I had prepared was consumed to the last morsel.

To that dinner, conceived in student gaiety and executed in utter innocence, may be traced a myth that, on occasion, has caused me considerable embarrassment. It was immediately bruited abroad that I was a chef of extraordinary resources, and that in the preparation of certain dishes I utilized the culinary secrets of the Borgias. Homes and apartments were placed at my disposal if only I would prepare a dinner for "a very select group." During the ensuing year I repeated the rabbit dish—I didn't dare attempt anything else!—forty or fifty times. Meanwhile I was trying desperately to live up to a reputation for which, I felt honestly, there was absolutely no foundation—except, possibly, a certain naïveté in my exceedingly enlightened friends. I systematized all the culinary knowledge that I had unconsciously absorbed as a reluctant apprentice in Mother's kitchen. I pestered with questions whoever I had reason to believe knew something about cookery. In short, I settled down more or less seriously—mostly less—to expand my sphere of culinary achievements.

The amiable professor of philosophy became my most effective press agent. As the years went by we became intimate friends. I cooked for him frequently and made his wine. When he went to meetings of philosophical societies, from coast to coast, he boasted to his astute colleagues that a vintner's son from the Chianti hills was in charge of his cellar. On at least one occasion he tucked the proof in his brief case and went across the continent to read a brilliant paper in defense of hedonism.

For reasons that will be discovered on the pages that follow, and implicit in the title to Part One of this book, I am suspicious of gourmets and connoisseurs, and so I resent being numbered among them. If someone suggests that I have "the artist's touch" in cookery, I swear that I shall feed him pork and beans with tinned spaghetti for dessert.

But despite my protestations, the myth that I am a chef has persisted. For the past several years my good friends have urged me to establish a restaurant. The more enthusiastic among them have suggested that I write a cookbook. The idea of becoming a restaurateur is wholly repugnant. The suggestion that I write a cookbook presupposes that I am either a cook or—heaven forbid!—a slavish plagiarist of untried recipes and perpetuator of culinary nonsense.

I love good food—as who does not? I take some pride in the fact that in the realm of gastronomy an unprejudiced palate is my only guide. Where I can't find food that pleases me, I fall to in the kitchen and prepare my own. Necessity has been the mother of what measure of invention and resourcefulness I possess in culinary matters. On occasion I produce something that smacks of real achievement. But I am not a cook. For example: I have never made an aspic salad, nor baked a pie.

However, the idea of writing a cookbook, after it had been suggested for a number of years, began to be somewhat alluring. Why not give it a try? An afternoon in my study, planning the chapters and writing out recipes, convinced me that the task would be unbearably dull. But perhaps I wasn't going at it in the right manner. So I spent the next few days examining critically the more popular, chatty volumes on cookery. It was during that time that I conceived the idea for the pages that follow.

II

Some of the books I examined are honest, pedestrian, unimaginative; some—very few—are honest and excellent. Others are coy, incredibly naïve little volumes that proclaim on every page in prose that repeatedly misses fire, the Oh-isn't-it-fun-to-eat philosophy. The most offensive, and in some cases the most popular, are those inspired by an unassimilated foreign cuisine. These are phony, impractical, misleading, and decadent. All of them—excepting the honest few—give the impression of being commercially inspired, designed to attract that remnant of the population that has not yet outlived the synthetic Bohemianism of the twenties. I concluded that what America needs is not another cookbook, but a book on bread and wine in relation to life.

What is the labored theme on the pages of these exuberant volumes? It is implicit in each of them that American cuisine is monotonously mediocre and by all odds the worst among civilized peoples—a generalization that leaves much to be desired by way of accuracy. Every one of these precious books on food is an imperative to the American housewife to clear her culinary affairs with Moscow, Shanghai, Rome, Berlin, and, preferably, Paris. The nod toward Paris is definitely in the imperative mood. So far as I know, no one has been sufficiently smug and reactionary to suggest that American cuisine is potentially the best, and that in certain quarters of this sprawling republic, American cookery is right in there pitching in the *cordon bleu* league. But of this, more anon.

It would be folly to deny that in general the American cook has much to learn from his Latin, Nordic, and Asiatic fellow in the realm of pots and pans; or that even every labor-bent peasant who crosses the terrifying Atlantic could add appreciably to the gaiety of the American executive's dinner hour. The difficulty is that those who have undertaken to teach the new world the culinary tricks of the old either do not understand, or consciously pervert, the meaning of bread and wine as ingredients in the good life. They are an articulate group—the exceptions are as rare as they are precious—of gastronomic adolescents who see this troubled life in terms of exotic sauces and unavailable vintages. Death to them is not the end of Life but the everlasting impossibility of smacking the lips and patting the bloated stomach.

They may be wiser. On the basis of what they write on food and drink they are the "Lost Generation" among kitchen knaves. They constitute *The Decadent Cult of Cookery.*

The American housewife who would venture beyond the limited orbit of tinned foods and watery pot roasts must seek her guide among this coterie of culinary expatriates. Their gastronomic Baedekers, potbellied and in chef's bonnet—the function of which, incidentally, is to keep dandruff and hair from falling into the soup—confront her in every bookstall in the nation. They have been prepared with synthetic urbanity by provincial Americans whose knowledge of food is essentially bookish and painfully self-conscious; by hack writers and tenth-rate novelists turned gourmets for the nonce to contribute their bit to the gaiety of the American dinner hour. From time to time their ranks are invaded by foreigners of questionable antecedents who, eager to do anything but honest work, capitalize on American naïveté by writing about the food and drink that, in another clime, sustained their useless lives.

No doubt they are all contributing something to America's gastronomic coming of age; but what little good they have done is offset by an evil from which at the moment no release is in sight, unless this revolt is effective beyond the writer's most unreasonable expectations. They have broadcast a dastardly falsehood, perhaps to give a certain status to their labor of love—that cooking is an *art.* The implication of all their dithyrambic spewings on culinary matters, despite their protestations to the contrary, is that excellent food and drink are achievements in refinement beyond the attainment of ordinary mortals. Some write in a mystic vein, and, with phony reverence—certainly with a disgustingly disproportionate sense of values—of little Burgundian villages where, one would suppose, people do nothing but eat and drink and exchange notes on the latest truffle hunt. They recall with appropriate drooling, and in atrocious prose, *cordon bleu* cooks (one must not say "blue ribbon," since it smacks of prize bulls at county fairs and so would break the incantation!) discovered in this or that cranny of the Alsatian countryside. With incredible impracticability they write of meats which marinate a fortnight and then simmer and seethe for hours and hours. Their recipes, fantastic enumerations of exotic ingredients bathed in quantities of cream and blends of liqueurs, are designed to frighten the most adventurous bride into eternal allegiance to ham and eggs.

Their unintended success in this is a sort of poetic justice. The American housewife has been convinced by these culinary fakirs that cooking is an art, and since she is at the moment in full revolt against the thesis that woman's place is in the home, she is quite willing to admit that her cooking isn't worth a damn —despite the spherical tendencies of her own and her mate's girth. She is in no mood to achieve distinction in the kitchen if to do so she must go snouting for truffles in the oak groves of Piedmont and preying upon snails in the vineyards of Burgundy. If cooking is an art, then by definition it can be mastered only by a select few—a conclusion which she has been quick to seize upon and to exploit in defense of her admitted ineptitude. If excellent meals require exotic and unavailable ingredients, endless hours in the kitchen, and a lifetime to perfect, Mrs. Jones is content to whet the can opener and concentrate on bridge.

But she cannot consistently ignore the call to culinary self-improvement. To meet special occasions she will now and then hazard an invasion of the sacred precincts. After a hectic shopping tour through the foreign sections, where she has discovered that many of the ingredients she had hoped to find flourish only between the covers of the cookery books she has been reading, she advances gaily into the kitchen and takes a snort of this or that—whichever she happens to have on hand—to bolster her morale and quicken the imagination. A survey of her pots and pans reveals that they are woefully inadequate. Quaking with a sense of impending failure, she begins to mince and sauté, simmer and strain. Her nerves kept in perfect equilibrium by her favorite cigarette, she meets each crisis as it emerges. Well in advance of the dinner hour, each little culinary symphony has received the final blessing, and the casseroles gurgle all over the stove. The guests arrive, and after such appropriate exclamations as "Oh, boy, am *I* hungry!" and "Doesn't something smell simply divine!" they light their cigarettes and settle down to guzzle quantities of whiskey and soda. When their palates are properly anesthetized they crowd around the dinner table and, amid laughter and corny ribaldry, stab uncertainly at the laden dishes. No one says a damned thing about the food—a fact which Mrs. Jones doesn't particularly notice, since she has done some pretty fair guzzling on her own account. But the morrow brings sober reflection—not to be confused with "emotion remembered in tranquillity"—and a reaffirmation of faith in watery pot roast, tinned string beans, and aspic salad.

III

Only the most complacent provincial would deny that American cuisine can be vastly improved; that— and this needs emphasis—the American's whole atti·

tude towards food and drink leaves much to be desired. The current demand for books on food and the
space devoted to culinary matters by the popular
magazines clearly indicate an increasing curiosity
about the quality of one's fare. It is also clear that
while on occasion the American enjoys Oriental and
Asiatic food, he prefers European cooking as a steady
diet, since it is more in harmony with his own basic
tradition. Furthermore, the ingredients of wholesome
European cookery are generally more available than
the Asiatic on the American market.

Those, however, who look to Europe for instruction
in cooking must studiously eschew the fakirs, the
gastronomic sensationalists, the apostles of culinary
decadence. Too often, the cuisine these immature
gourmets write about is precious and extravagant. It
is the cuisine of the idle rich, foreign and domestic,
designed to give new thrills and new excitements to
pitiful souls who have never known the enduring joy
of an honest, productive life. It is the cuisine of con-
secutive courses, accompanied by a variety of wines,
white and red, still and sparkling, followed by exotic
desserts and an array of liqueurs.

What the American housewife needs, first of all,
is to formulate a sensible attitude toward food and
drink; to see the dinner hour in perspective, as an
element in the good life. She needs next, not recipes
under baffling, foreign names, but rather some basic
culinary ideas to aid her in making judicious use of
the extraordinary quantity and variety of materials
at her disposal. For valuable guidance in the preparation of inexpensive and distinguished fare, she could
do worse than look to the European mother who,
perhaps unhappily, has no illusions about her proper
place and function. The ultimate goal here should
be the perfection of a native cuisine, varied and en-

riched by the culinary ideas brought to us by our immigrants from the four corners of the world.

The question of nationality in food is relatively unimportant. Throughout Europe the basic philosophy of its preparation is identical. It is a philosophy of cookery rooted in necessity, and like most philosophies of such origin, it is wholly sound. Across the years the European has devised a method for turning humble ingredients into dishes that can be eaten with relish; when the method is applied to choice basic substances, the results are accordingly distinguished. *Risotto* is a typically Milanese dish because the rice fields and the dairy products are near by; but it is also found in other Latin countries with such slight differences in preparation as are made necessary by the availability of ingredients.

It is idle to insist that the mature cuisine of one country is better than the equally mature cuisine of another. French cookery is generally preferred to all others for no better reason, I think, than that, as in all things else where coteries and cults seem to be the fashion, the French have seized and never relinquished the initiative. Some prefer the Italian because its pretensions are modest and worth achieving, while its happy blending of the leguminous and the farinaceous, the emphasis on green vegetables, and the sparing use of meats, make it eminently satisfying as a steady diet. Good food, no matter whence it comes, should be enjoyed with gratitude and thanksgiving. Personally, I take some pride in the fact that in culinary matters I was an internationalist long before the Atomic Age. I will retreat from no dish that pleases an unprejudiced though somewhat aristocratic palate.

So whether one chooses to follow the French or the Italian, the Nordics or the Asiatics, is of little importance; the basic principle in the achievement of good living is a sane, wholesome attitude toward food and drink. One must avoid the extremes of decadence and indifference. The decadent's furor must be cooled by reminding him that man does not live by bread alone, while the indifferent who takes such pitiful pride in the boast that all food is the same to him should be reminded that his uncritical culinary tolerance will make him prematurely old and grumpy. Nothing is so effective in keeping one young and full of lust as a discriminating palate thoroughly satisfied at least once a day.

An accomplished cuisine is only one of the ingredients in the good life. It is perhaps the basic ingredient; but to look upon it as either more or less than that is to pervert its meaning. Man should enjoy his meals as much as he enjoys his work, his friends, his favorite recreation. And he *will* enjoy them once he discovers how pleasant the business of nourishing oneself can be. Generalizations in such matters are hazardous, but there is enough plausibility in the statement that one who approaches the dinner table glowing with the anticipation of good food—and ready to raise hell if it isn't—usually exhibits the same zest for other phases of life also. The hearty, discriminating eater is seldom a sour puss. He does not live to eat; rather, he eats well and drinks judiciously, that he may pursue his interests in life with greater enthusiasm. His sense of proportion is admirable. He considers a restful bed as important as a good dinner, and a comfortable chair and adequate lamp to read by as necessary as after-dinner coffee and brandy. He knows, too, that simplicity and variety, both in ingredients and in their preparation, are the abiding principles on which the distinguished diet is based. A cup of broth, fine, crisp bread, good cheese, celery and chicory hearts, a bottle of wine—never mind the French names and ancient vintages—topped with coffee and brandy, make a pleasant and satisfying dinner.

While economy may be a consequence, it is totally irrelevant to the principle of simplicity and variety as a guide in distinguished cookery; the principle rests on purely gastronomic considerations. Simple fare enhances the enjoyment of the more refined, which should be reserved for all festive occasions. Continuous indulgence in rich sauces, prime meats and fowl, elaborate desserts, rare wines and liqueurs, leads to jaded appetites, an increasing inability to enjoy the dinner hour, and—to gout.

I was frequently puzzled as a child by the simple dinners Mother prepared for wealthy Italians who came to our country home from the city. They came usually in the spring or fall. We had, on those occasions, what seemed to me strangely simple fare for such distinguished guests. Always we began the meal with a fine broth, usually with fresh escarole cooked in it a few minutes before serving, followed by boiled beef and quantities of cooked turnip greens and dandelion salad. Wine, cheese, and an immense amount of homemade bread rounded out the meal. Now I understand. Those men were true gourmets; they came to the country for what they had missed in the city.

I recall another incident, which is perhaps not to the point but worth relating nevertheless. In the little Tuscan village where I was born was a rosy-cheeked, corpulent clergyman, a notoriously hearty eater. When he came to our home for dinner on a certain occasion, Mother had severely taxed a meager budget in order to roast a capon. While we were eating a vegetable soup, the clergyman remarked, with what even to my child's mind seemed misplaced piety, that

we peasants were fortunate in being obliged by circumstances to eat such an abundance of vegetables
My father, who had his own reasons for being unen-
thusiastic about clergymen, immediately ordered
Mother to comply with the implied request of our
visitor. Accordingly, the clergyman's plate was heaped
with greens, raw and cooked, while the rest of us
dispatched the fowl with extraordinary gusto. I do
not know to this day with what relish our pious guest
satisfied his inordinate appetite. I suspect that my
father knew what he was doing.

We shall have come to our culinary senses when we
have banished from our vocabulary the misleading
phrase "the art of cooking," and thus shown as much
sense of propriety as Alexis Soyer, the great French
chef of the past century. One day while in a library,
he noticed among the works of Shakespeare a book
with the vague inscription "Nineteenth Edition."
Upon turning to the first page he was horrified to discover a recipe for making oxtail soup. When later he
wrote his own cookbook he begged the reader under
no circumstances to place it on the same shelf with
Paradise Lost.

Viewed in perspective, cooking is a routine household duty no more difficult to perform with distinction than keeping the home tidy and attractive, the
children clean, well-behaved, and happy—all tasks
which the American mother does well and with justifiable pride. Both men and women can learn to
cook with equal competence. If men occasionally ex-
cel, it is because to them it is either an exclusive occupation or an avocation; while the woman must too
frequently cook amid the numerous and unpredictable
distractions that constitute the indivisible legacy of
motherhood. As in all things else, some do the job

with more imagination, more finesse, and greater gusto; but all can learn to do it with competence.

And this last is of basic importance. So, away with the Brillat-Savarins and their culinary refinement. Banish unintelligible menus and exotic ingredients. Scorn the hack writers turned gourmets. Learn a few basic principles and get a firm grip on this solid, heartening fact: the American housewife—man or woman—is potentially the best of all possible cooks; for even in times of scarcity—the use of that word as descriptive of American economy at any time would horrify the contemporary European—she has in shameful abundance all the necessary ingredients. She lives in a veritable paradise of flesh, fish, and fowl, of fruits, vegetables, and dairy products; while the great transoceanic airliners bring to her market all the condiments and ingredients not indigenous to the region in which she lives. All she needs is the will to take advantage of her opportunities. For the increased joy of her precious brood, may she do so with all speed.

2

The Discovery
of Abundance

WHAT IS the purpose of life? Man was placed upon the earth for what reason? To do what? To accomplish what ends? Ask contemporary philosophers these questions and you will merely renew an old controversy. If you had asked me when I was ten years old, my answer would have been prompt and unambiguous: Work is the purpose of life. Man was placed upon the earth to discover how difficult it is to provide for the simple needs of the body.

This is not a philosophy in retrospect. It was the credo of which I was most certain at the age when the American boy sees life in terms of end runs, outside curves, and the vulgar falsehoods of the cinema. I could not possibly have avoided the lesson. Parents and grandparents drove it home with patience, exasperation, and, where these means failed, with the appropriate weapon. The teacher repeated it at school. The stories read in the successive readers glorified work and urged its necessity. The parish priest could find little else to say to me than that I should be a good boy, obey my parents, and do the will of God. The pious formula meant simply work.

Even the Santa Claus myth—or rather its Italian equivalent—was intimately related to labor. *La Befana* came on the eve before Epiphany (January 6) to distribute gifts to children. But there was a condition. According to the myth, the kindly old hag would arrive at the home chilled to the marrow and insist, of course, on being warmed before she filled the stockings. She would also want to be assured that the children had gathered enough fuel to see the family through the winter.

And you may be sure that they had, since each one eagerly awaited the feast of the Epiphany. From the close of the harvest season through the end of the year, children competed with each other for the remnants of fuel left scattered on the barren landscape by the more opulent landowners who expected the infant gleaners. The pruned vineyards, after the owner had gathered the larger clippings, were the favorite hunting grounds. Chips from felled trees, corncobs, and twigs were put into the mendicant's bag and taken home. Occasionally—and what a prize that was considered!—a farmer could be cajoled by an engaging lad to part with the trunk and roots of a small tree that he had cut down.

The reward for months of labor and anxiety was modest and immensely satisfying. No toys! There would have been no time to play with them anyway. The typical contents of the stocking were a pine cone about a foot long and filled with nuts, an orange, some filberts, and a pound or so of walnuts and chestnuts. And a bit of confection if the family could afford it. All edibles!

The work routine was neither exhausting nor beyond the child's strength and endurance. It was simply continuous and left little time to play. In addition to gathering fuel, he was expected to help till the soil, feed the animals and keep them clean, earn an odd penny in a variety of ways, and assist in the care of younger brothers and sisters. The terror of scarcity kept everyone, old and young alike, soberly at his assigned duties.

In comparison, the average American enjoys inexhaustible abundance. Nevertheless, he complains. And that is understandable. His means are not always adequate to satisfy the needs which a prodigal environment has made habitually extravagant, while even during those annoying periods of economic recession, when everyone is patiently waiting for prosperity to round the corner, he has infrequently known the meaning of *real* scarcity.

He is right, of course, in his efforts continuously to improve his circumstances, and in his insistence upon a more equitable share of his community's unequaled resources. He is not impressed by the assurance that, compared with that of the starving millions in Europe and Asia, his pantry is a gourmet's paradise. He appraises his stock of worldly goods in terms of America's fantastic wealth, and he is not satisfied with less than what he considers his proper share.

But while he struggles to attain more, he must learn to make the most of what he has; and if he is willing to learn how to live well on what is immediately available to him, his best bet is to look to the immigrant for advice. No one in this land of cattle ranges and wheat fields appreciates more profoundly the meaning of *abundance* than the immigrant who came here in search of bread. He left the old country, not to seek new opportunities—that word has a typically American meaning, unintelligible to the immigrant until he becomes Americanized—but because he had reached the point of despair in a country where continuous backbreaking labor was wholly futile; where the fruit of one's toil was never quite adequate to replenish the energy expended in its achievement. And so he came here because he had been told that his labor would yield bread—tons of *white* bread. I know because I was one of them.

To be sure, I found much more. Father had been here for several years employed by a logging and milling company. When he had established a home and called his family to America, I had assumed, plausibly, that I would help him bring the trees from the forest to the mill. When upon reaching the West Coast I saw the size of the trees, I resigned myself to the requirements of the law and went, somewhat reluctantly, to school. Had someone suggested that the great public school system was at my disposal, that I would receive its benefits from the first grade through the university, that someday I should be writing books in that baffling language which I was certain I should never learn, I would have thought him a completely irresponsible lunatic. In fact, no one did suggest it— not even Father, who was passionately devoted to learning. The family was large, the needs urgent; and so it was taken for granted that in two or three years I would begin my apprenticeship in the woods as a "whistle punk." Personally, I was impatient to answer the call of the forest, to get to work like a man and to contribute to the support of the family.

But things worked out differently—and happily. A succession of kindly, understanding teachers made the task of learning the language much more pleasant than I had supposed was possible. The elementary grades were quickly ingested; high school—and football—became increasingly alluring . . . But that, and much more, are matter for another volume. I am here concerned with the story of the immigrant's discovery of abundance, a story that will help to explain much that follows and, perhaps, make the American housewife aware of the culinary possibilities within her grasp.

When I was a youngster in Italy, before the ravages of Fascism and war, the return of an emigrant to his native village was a gay event in which the whole community shared. What with his fine woolen garments, amazingly handsome shoes of real leather, his bleached complexion and smooth hands, and the strange, unintelligible phrases with which he peppered his speech, the man himself seemed wholly transformed. The fantastic stories he had to tell about America—no one believed them, but all listened with incredible eagerness—absorbed the community's interest for months after his return. They were true stories, as I was later to discover for myself, and told only with that degree of exaggeration endemic in the race; stories of tree trunks so large that several couples might dance upon them without getting in each other's way; of wheat fields so vast that no fast train could traverse them in a single day; of meats and sweets and fine clothes so universally enjoyed that it was impossible to distinguish the rich from the poor. And of incredible waste! No American, he would assure his fellow peasants, ever eats an entire sandwich; he always throws away the fringe of crust.

But of immediate interest to the villagers was the emigrant's trunk, for it was crammed full of sweets. The most prized were the chocolate bars, and absolutely the most bewildering was the chewing gum. No one could ever quite believe the fantastic explanation that the stuff was to be chewed but not swallowed. However, the temptation to ingest the strange delicacy was bravely resisted when we were told that if it ever got to the stomach, it would mean a cementing of the bowels and certain death. And so the little rectangular bars were rationed, distributed, and dutifully masticated. We took turns chewing and passing on the remains from hungry mouth to hungry mouth until there was nothing left. The little rations of chocolate were hoarded and nibbled from time to time to re-lieve the monotonous taste of stale and moldy bread.

Our enthusiasm for the sweets brought by the re-turned emigrant was understandable. Sugar among the peasants was so scarce as to be virtually unavail-able, and the body's normal craving for it went un-satisfied except for an occasional tart made with chest-nutmeal in the winter. Fruit, such as figs, grapes, and peaches in season, was the only other source of sugar. And they too were eaten sparingly, since even those who grew them had to sell them in order to buy basic necessities. I remember many occasions on which I was threatened and cudgeled for a crime no more serious than plucking a cluster of grapes from the roadside vine. And that in a land where grapes are grown in abundance! But when I came to America I had my revenge on the misfortune of birth. Within six months I had eaten enough sweets to supply my body with sugar for a full century. I have eaten none since.

Fynes Moryson, the Elizabethan traveler and Lin-colnshire gentleman, observed long ago that the "Ital-ian will eat a charger full of herbs and roots with three pennyworth of bread" and thus satisfy his appe-tite. Times have not changed much since the Renais-sance, except recently—and for the worse. The pre-vailing notion in America that Italians subsist on spaghetti smothered in rich meat sauces and grated cheese, while it may describe the Neapolitan's dream of paradise, is entirely mistaken. Farinaceous and le-guminous products have long been the staples there, but there is much more to spaghetti than a kettle full of boiled paste. The scarcity of meat and cheese has made that hearty dish distinctly holiday fare. The Italian still draws heavily on root and leaf vegetables for relief from a diet of beans and grain products:

and Moryson's observation must be construed as meaning that the Italian is a vegetarian by necessity and
not by choice.

I would hesitate to designate any one dish as basic
in the Italian's diet. All food there is scarce, and the
day-to-day fare for the masses is extraordinarily simple. Bread is eaten in quantities in every region. It is
eaten with onions, with a little cheese or ham, with
fresh fruit or cured fish—with anything available that
will help to make it more palatable. Thick soups, peasant soups, with a bean base and plenty of vegetables
are eaten three times daily during the season when
the necessary ingredients are found in abundance.
Bean and vegetable broths are used universally when
the bread, which is baked at infrequent intervals in
order to economize on fuel, is so hard and stale that
it must be soaked in soup to make it edible. In the
spring and summer, quantities of vegetables, both
raw and cooked, with and without condiment, are
consumed throughout the peninsula. In a little village
in the north during World War I, the entire population was stricken with a terrible disease as a result of
eating greens picked in a pasture where the enemy's
horses had grazed. The diet changes from season to
season and from region to region; everywhere it reflects what can be extracted from the earth and the
water without recourse to the general market.

If there is any one dish—aside from paste, which is
so widely used in soups—eaten in greater quantities
than any other, it is *polenta*. North of Rome, in Tuscany, in Lombardy, in Piedmont, and in the Venetian
provinces, this thick, coarse, corn-meal mush is always on the table. The metropolitan American knows
it as the elegant dish served in Italian restaurants in
Boston, New York, and San Francisco. Or perhaps he
has eaten it at the home of his Italian friends, served

with casserole rabbit or chicken and mushrooms. Excellent fare, superb when served with rich, red wine; but such is not the *polenta* as eaten by the Italian peasant! Of course, the mush itself, since it is nothing more than corn meal cooked in water, is the same anywhere, though the grind and the quality of the corn make some difference; but the condiment, the fowl, the mushrooms, the rich sauce—these the Italian has found in America, and with them a means for transmuting a dish which in his native land had become obnoxious to him.

The culinary inventiveness of the Italian housewife, as I well remember, was severely taxed in devising means to make such humble fare attractive to her children. Except on rare occasions, as rare as they were memorable, the best she could do was to smother it with salt cod baked in tomato sauce. Everywhere she was frustrated by lack of ingredients. And so we ate it hot with cream cheese, or with turnip greens cooked and sprinkled with a miserly dash of olive oil, or with hot cracklings, and a thousand other lowly auxiliaries. We ate it cold with figs and grapes, with green onions and cheese. We buried it in bowls of bean broth and cabbage. We sliced it and grilled or fried the stuff with indifferent results. It was, it remained, always and forever—*polenta,* a veritable plague, an evil from which no deliverance seemed possible. We had not yet thought seriously of America.

But of all the miserable bait with which we were lured into eating more and more of that insipid and bloating yellow nightmare, the lowly pilchard was positively the worst. I do not know how pilchards were cured, nor do I care. They came pressed beyond recognition in barrels; ugly, foul, putrefied little creatures from the Mediterranean. The perverse genius of the race, the evil inventiveness of the Borgias and the

Medicis, the hatred of the Guelfs and Ghibellines have coalesced in the pilchard barrel of the Italian grocery store. When I was dispatched to the grocer's to buy a brace of the little critters, I knew what lay in store. On the way home I gouged out their eyes and ate them out of sheer spite, cursing the while in a manner shockingly precocious in one so young. At home they were broiled on live coals, sprinkled with olive oil, and placed in a platter on the center of the table. Then each member of the family would take his turn dabbing pieces of *polenta* on the fish—gentle little taps, just enough to soak up the stench. When the stomach was about full, the fish was divided among the members of the happy family, each to do with his share as he wished. That is to say, to eat it and thank God for another bellyful.

I frequently complained, in the innocent manner of children who have yet to learn that their misery cannot always be interpreted in terms of parental discipline, and asked why we had to eat such awful stuff. My grandfather, who preferred bread dunked in wine —which he had regularly for breakfast until his eighty-eighth year, when he died prematurely of snakebite— sought to console me on such occasions by telling me what *he* had had to eat when *he* was a boy. The sermon was his version of the familiar one which has left grandchildren grumbling since the first grandfather mumbled it in his beard. His fare, he assured me, had been the same *polenta*, served with the same befouled Mediterranean pilchard, but with this miserable difference: after the fish had been warmed over the coals, his mother suspended it on a string from the ceiling so that it hovered over the center of the table. Then each member of the family would tap it gaily with his piece of *polenta*, sending it with deft strokes

across the way to his brother or sister who promptly
returned the compliment. And thus amid peals of
laughter and bacchanalian revelry, each filled his
belly and concluded with a prayer for a bumper crop
of yellow corn. That done, the pilchard, somewhat
frayed but none the worse for wear, was ceremo-
niously detached from the string, wrapped securely
in wax paper, and stored in the pantry to await the
morrow's eager barrage of *polenta*. When completely
worn out, it was replaced by another, more foul and
evil-smelling. Grandfather was a grand old man.

II

Fed on this meager and monotonous fare, hungry
for white bread, coffee, and sugar, flesh and fowl, I
came to America. Against the background of pilchards
and *polenta*, what I found here, in this land of refu-
gees from hunger and oppression, remains for me a
dramatic and ever fascinating story. I found, first of
all, the meaning, the consumable, edible meaning, of
a simple word, lost in the dictionary among thousands
of others—the meaning of the word *abundance*. I had
known scarcity, had lived on intimate terms with its
agonizing reality; and the discovery of its opposite,
its annihilator, was an experience so maddening with
joy, so awful and bewildering, that I am not yet fully
recovered from the initial shock. Give man bread,
woolens against the cold, labor that he enjoys, and
you may open wide the doors to the futile agitator of
riots and revolutions. While it may be no longer true
that an army marches on its stomach, it is everlast-
ingly true that a social order endures so long as the
pantries of its citizens are stocked with good food.
Thus food, bread and meat in sinful profusion, was

my first discovery; and after that I came to know what I can best describe as the naturalization of Italian cuisine.

When I arrived in America, I recalled and immediately understood a saying I had frequently heard in Italy. When one had met with a bit of good fortune, such as an unusual yield from the vine or perhaps a meager inheritance, his friends would say to him, "*Eh, l'hai trovata l'America!*" Ha, you have found your America. This expression, in various dialectical versions, is current among Italian immigrants in America even today.

I was not immediately impressed by the skyscrapers, the automobiles, and the roaring trains of the metropolitan centers along the eastern seaboard. The only emotion they stirred within me was fear—fear of being lost, engulfed, annihilated. What *was* immediately impressive were the food stalls; the huge displays of pastries and confections, the mountains of fish, flesh, and fowl; the crowded cafés, where the aristocrat—or so he seemed—sat beside the drayman in overalls, gulping coffee drawn from huge urns and soberly eating ham and eggs; eating such fare without any visible display of joy, as if in obedience to some distasteful duty—as if it were yesterday's *polenta!* Ham and eggs! (Come to your senses, ye brave Americans, and spare your noble dish the corrupting catsup! Amend your constitution—you did it once against misguided gourmets—that you may enjoin forever such culinary adultery.) Ham and eggs with fried potatoes, stacks of buttered toast and coffee—that was my first acquaintance with American food. It remains to this day my favorite American dish. I would pay dearly for a gulp-to-gulp moving picture of myself, seated in a New York restaurant, a hungry immigrant urchin to the core, trying to counterfeit nonchalance as

I wolfed my culinary cares away. And as I remembered the boot of earth across the water, where eggs had been too precious to be served with any regularity, and where coffee had been hoarded against the bellyache—its curative value somehow mysteriously related to its scarcity—I said to myself, *"L'America é buona."* America is good.

Several years later I heard those identical words spoken by an Italian grocer to whom I had gone for provisions. It was in one of those intimate shops, none too tidy, crowded with sacks of beans, peas, lentils, *ceci*, barrels of olives, huge wheels of cheese and stacks of *salami* and dry cod, where the opulent and inefficient operator is more ready to chat than to sell. He took me into his dingy office, rolled back the top of some late executive's desk, as if he were about to show me his ledger or perhaps a recent issue of *Practical Merchandising*, and revealed loaves of bread, slabs of cheese, and several *salami*. He then pulled out a drawer, which in any sensible establishment would have catapulted a typewriter into view, and several bottles of wine emerged from the darkness. He locked the door to the establishment, sliced the *salame*, uncorked a bottle, and opened a can of olives. As he sat down and reached for the cheese, he mumbled, in his own version of the English language, "America ees gude. Today, leet the *paesani* spend the mawney in the safetyway store."

I left New York for the West Coast during the harvest season. As the train raced westward, the prodigality of America unfolded in a series of beatific visions, marred, alas! by bewildering disappointments. Somewhere along the way, the train skirted an apple orchard. Apples were heaped upon the ground in veritable mountains—or so it appeared at the time to my eager fancy. Perhaps there had been an unusual storm; perhaps they had been shaken down to be carted away to the cider mill. Or were they actually abandoned to rot on the ground? I had no way of knowing. Whatever the reason, there they were, in unguarded profusion and apparently available to anyone. There were no farmers lurking with clubs and pruning hooks among the trees, as I had seen them in Italy, ready to ward off sugar-hungry lads who might be tempted by the ripe fruit. As we continued our journey, I added apples to my blessings.

There were, as I have said, disappointments. The food distributed to immigrants on the train and at railway stations was awful. It was sold in box lunches that contained sandwiches of *salame* and cheese. There were also oranges, bananas, and apples. The bread was suspiciously white, moist, tasteless, and it stuck to the teeth. The *salame* was completely phony. It was a dry, rancid, foul-smelling substance parading under an honorable name. The cheese, a sickly-yellow mess, was positively revolting. The oranges were sour, the apples large, mealy, and without flavor. The bananas were so totally unfamiliar, both in appearance and taste, that I approached them with misgivings. I learned to like them, but it took a little time. Ham and eggs I never saw again until I reached the West Coast. Somewhere along the way I found enough French bread to take care of my needs for the remainder of the journey. I had grave doubts about the quality of such American food as bread, *salame*, and cheese, but I reserved final judgment. There is no need to hold back any longer. The bread is worse now than it was then, since the great baking trusts have become more adept at perverting wheat flour. American salami is still a stinker in disguise. The yellow counterfeit for cheese is still extant, though one may now find cheeses of excellent quality manufactured according to European formulas. American fruit would be comparable to any other if it were left on the tree long enough to ripen. I suspect that it would have more flavor if the Burbanks had plied their trade with a little less zeal and if water were used more sparingly in the orchards.

When I arrived at what was to be my future home in Washington, I realized the full meaning of America in terms of food, clothing, and shelter. Everyone ate quantities of meat, pastries, and fruit. Everyone was well-dressed. Everyone bought wood for the cookstove though he lived in the midst of a forest where wood was rotting on the ground. To a lad who had combed the countryside in Italy in search of sticks and corncobs for fuel, this latter fact was shocking and unintelligible. Even to this day the forests of the Pacific Coast have an immediate significance for me of which the natives are totally unaware. When I drive to the hills for an outing I cannot resist the ancient urge. So I never leave the woods without first filling the trunk with wood for the fireplace.

During the first few months in America I went to the forest every day and returned home laden with its precious fruit. There were nuts and berries in profusion. With my father I hunted grouse, pheasant, quail, and rabbit. Here and there were abandoned homesteads with pear, plum, and apple orchards. The reality was more fantastic than the dream. What the returned natives had reported about America proved to be entirely accurate. It seemed possible to live on the prodigal yield of the surrounding hills. Although we all worked hard in our eagerness to take advantage of new opportunities, we did not neglect what was to be had for no more effort than was required in gathering it. We never bought a bit of fuel. A variety of game from the forest provided much of our meat for the dinner table. The cellar was always well stocked with jams, jellies, nuts, and fruit gathered in the woods and abandoned orchards. And while we were gradually becoming naturalized and eagerly looking forward to citizenship, we were also naturalizing our cuisine. We were realizing its potentialities in a land where we were no longer frustrated by scarcity and lack of variety.

The sinful waste among the native population left me amazed and horrified. On the school grounds, and later in the mills and lumber camps, I discovered the American's disrespect for food. Old and young alike drew from their lunch buckets huge sandwiches of homemade bread filled with meats, jams, and precious butter. They took large bites from the centers and threw irreverently upon the ground "the fringe of crust." The slabs of apple and raisin pie, prepared with so much care by Grandmother—grandmothers always make the best pies—were seldom entirely eaten. Only a few ate the neatly folded flaky crust at the edge.

In view of what I later heard women say about making piecrust, this fact convinced me that the ways of the American, as of the Almighty, are inscrutable. Women either apologize for, or take inordinate pride in, their pies. The only reason which makes any sense at all, why Grandmother's pie is so universally acclaimed, is that pie-making is a process which requires a lifetime to perfect. Since anyone can slice apples, the secret must lie in making the crust. I have never heard women discussing new techniques for slicing apples, though I have heard them a thousand times inquiring of each other how to make a good crust. Tell me, then, why even Grandmother's crust, perfected after three score years of study, toil, and kitchen gossip, should be ignominiously thrown into the slop pail!

III

The account of my discovery of abundance summarizes an experience in which millions of immigrants to America have shared. The overwhelming majority of them, from northern and southern Europe, from the Balkans and the Near East, have found a new felicity here basically explainable in terms of bread. They have brought to this prodigal land a profound respect for everything that the native takes for granted. Their frugal habits, their willingness to work, their resourcefulness in meeting adversity, explain why their names appear so infrequently on relief roles. Their culinary aptitudes, evolved in scarcity and a bleak environment as a means of turning nothing into something, when applied even to the most modest ingredients available to them here, yields a consistently distinguished cuisine. Man for man and dollar for dollar, the immigrants' daily fare is several degrees of excellence higher than that of the natives. They have evolved what can be defined only as a naturalized cuisine. In all the population of America, they are the most satisfied, the most gay, and the least neurotic.

Except for the tenement districts of the more dehumanized industrial centers, where one is completely victimized by the immediate environment, go wherever you wish and observe how the immigrant lives. He will be found most frequently below the tracks in very modest quarters, none too tidy on the outside. It will be found, as expected, that he has much to learn about cleanliness and sanitation. The available space of earth is usually planted, with professional skill, in vegetables rather than in flowers. (The second generation is grumbling effectively about this, and soon beans will give way to roses.) Where wood and coal are the prevailing fuel, these will be stacked or piled in the yard against the winter season. Since life below the tracks is admittedly less civilized, there will be rabbit hutches and chicken coops.

The furniture in the home, except for the gaudy upholstered pieces in the parlor, reserved strictly for company, will be simple and inexpensive. The floor will be covered with linoleum rather than costly carpets. (If the Americanized children grumble about this, as indeed they do, they will be reminded by their mother that Americans have well-carpeted floors and mush in the pantry. As likely as not she will brandish a luscious Torino *salame* while she drives home the point.) The cellar will be stocked with wine, produce from the garden, and mushrooms from the hills and golf courses. There will be cases of oil, wheels of cheese, and a variety of cured meats, along with the ubiquitous paste in all conceivable patterns.

Everywhere is unmistakable evidence that the immigrant prizes substance above form, food and comfort to meaningless ostentation; that he cuddles up very close to life. The dinner is prepared to be eaten and not to dazzle the eye as in the manner of food illustrations in the slicks. It is simply served and with a minimum of implements. The bread is good, and butter will not recoil from it in disgust as it does from the sliced impostor sold by the baking combines. The soup is made from sound, flavored stock; the roast, flavored with herbs and larded with olive oil, mounts to the nostrils and invites to the feast; the vegetables, simmered in meat juices, bear no resemblance to their watery kin served above the tracks. The cheese is real rather than "type." The wine is clear, rich, and thoroughly honest. The glasses in which it is served were designed for men with large, rough hands and good stomachs.

Day in and day out, such is the immigrant's fare in America. It is consistently good because, in a land of plenty, he has set his standards of self-nourishment high. He subsidizes his fluctuating income by wringing from his environment all that it will yield. He will forgo the motorcar and the movies that he may increase the quality of his bread and wine. Regardless of his means, he will garden his plot of ground because he knows the vital difference between cold storage or tinned peas and those plucked from the vine an hour before they are eaten. Furthermore, challenging the soil for its produce is in his bones; the pleasure of eating what he raises is inseparably fused with the pleasure of raising what he eats. But it all adds up to a gay life, a life rooted in earth.

Along with himself, he has naturalized his cuisine. With satisfying results he applies the culinary tricks of the old world to the produce of the new. He has abandoned the eel, the frog, the snail, the swallows and meadow larks whose nests he haunted with avidity; and while he refers to such dainties with pardonable sentiment, since he enjoyed them so infrequently and at such sacrifice, he now concentrates his talents on beef, pork, lamb, and fowl. He eats *polenta* frequently, wholly transformed with rabbit or fowl and meaty mushroom sauces. Old habits and attitudes persist, however, and he apologizes when he serves it to his friends. He also eats quantities of dandelion salad, but whereas in the old country he ate it as a main course with bread, or perhaps with a bit of cheese, here it is the pleasant accompaniment to roast flesh or fowl. His dinner table is seldom without cooked leafy vegetables, such as mustard and turnip greens, cabbage and kale, spinach and chard. The Italian eats them in amazing portions with the appropriate meat dishes; and always, of course, they have been cooked in generous quantities of olive oil and butter, or blanched, then simmered in the flavored meat juices of the roast—or in many other appetizing ways made possible by America's contribution to his good life.

And what he has found here is available in even greater abundance to the American middle-class family. I repeat that the American housewife is potentially the best cook in the world; for she has the finest equipment, the most amazing culinary conveniences, and the widest possible latitude in the choice of raw materials. All she needs is to bring to the preparation of food the same talent, the same degree of imagination, the same care that she devotes daily to other household duties. It is all a matter of the proper attitude.

There is a simple, enduring joy—and it needs to be discovered—implicit in the preparation of such excellent dinners that Father and the children would deem it a grave misfortune to miss one of them. It is the solid, thoroughly human satisfaction derived from doing something which inspires admiration while it promotes the happiness of others. In some ways she has already achieved distinction as a cook. American fried chicken is difficult to surpass. There is no one who can compete with the American mother in the variety and excellence of desserts. The American breakfast, an ingenious combination of fruit, cereal, eggs with bacon or ham, and the finest coffee found anywhere, is a superb culinary achievement. This is all a brilliant beginning. Why not enjoy going the whole way?

3

The Things My Fathers
Used to Do

"THREE YARDS of manure. Well! you are going to America. Well! And you are leaving tomorrow afternoon. Well!" He took a handful, felt its texture between the finger tips, raised it to the nostrils. "Young man, you have polluted this with fillers. I can still smell the hay and the straw. But since you are going far away, never to return, I'll be generous with you. How about thirty-five cents?"

He was a shrewd peasant and I a shrewd lad. We both knew that notwithstanding the straw and the hay in it, the manure was worth a dollar. But he had me on the hip, and so I was obliged to liquidate my assets at a sacrifice before leaving for my new home, one-fourth the distance around the world.

He was right. I had mixed considerable hay and straw with the cow pats and horse dumplings; but since my original plan had been to sell the manure the following spring, by which time the fillers would have been completely rotted, my conduct had not been entirely dishonorable. It was just my tough luck that I had to sell before my scheme had thoroughly ripened.

The proper inference from this is that I was skilled in the techniques of free enterprise long before I had been told that it is synonymous with The American

Way of Life. So much so, indeed, that I might say I was Americanized before I had even thought of coming to America. Furthermore, I had the makings of a solid American on other grounds. My origins were no less humble than Lincoln's. He got his start in life splitting rails; I got mine gathering manure on the highway. He went on to become our most distinguished president, the Great Liberator, the author of the Gettysburg Address. From gathering manure I went on to America, to a new way of life, to teaching eager youth. The parallel is not wholly facetious.

But let me go back to my free-enterprising childhood that I may explain how, on the eve of my departure for the New World, I had accumulated assets liquidated at thirty-five cents. As befits an enterpriser of heroic caliber, I always had several projects under way; but gathering manure was the most exciting, if not the most profitable. Moreover, it was highly competitive—not simply in theory, but in fact. There were no secret agreements among the gleaners of manure, no hidden combines plying their trade behind the façade of a plausible formula. The competitors worked shoulder to shoulder in an undertaking that afforded excellent opportunity for the development of shrewdness, an attribute central in all business success.

On Wednesdays and Saturdays the peasants drove their livestock to market for barter, sale, or exchange. Early in the morning on these days, we children of the neighborhood went to the highway with shovels and hand-drawn carts to await the driven animals—cows, horses, mules, sheep, and goats. For obvious reasons we preferred the larger animals, and when a goodly number came by, we shadowed their tails.

In all competitive undertakings there are rules and regulations, and we had our own. It is axiomatic, of course, that cow pats and horse dumplings cannot be gathered, even by the most zealous enterpriser, until the animals see fit to release them. When the release occurred, it presented a problem: who, of the twelve or so gleaners was to have them? If all rushed for the booty in a mad scramble, the likely result would have been broken skulls and almost certainly total waste of the product. We had had no course in economics to guide us, but I think our disposition of the problem was entirely fair. When the animals came by, each lad chose the one—or more, depending on the size of the herd—he thought would most likely relieve himself within a reasonable time. There were empirical grounds on which the choice could be made, as I suppose there are objective data to guide one who dabbles in stocks and bonds. And, of course, the shrewd lad who knew best the intimate habits of horses and cattle always came out on top of the heap.

One could tell, for example, by a careful examination of the rump, tail, and legs of the animal, whether he had recently relieved himself of yesterday's hay. Under the circumstances, unfortunately, the test was not always reliable, since the peasants were also shrewd and kept their cattle clean for the market. Furthermore, in anticipation of market day, some of the animals had been fed grain and hay rather than grass, a diet that normally results in solid evacuation, neatly deposited and with no telltale traces.

The shrewd manure gatherer knew also that cows and horses frequently give certain premonitory signs before they do the deed. There is a perceptible hesitation in the jaunty stride, a slight hunching of the back, a characteristic restlessness in the tail, and successive dilations and contractions in the visible part of the organ involved. Unfortunately, these signs were not always reliable, since on occasion they turned out to be overelaborate preambles to an absolutely noncollectable puff of wind. However, an animal who went through such maneuvers, we all knew, bore diligent watching.

The clever boys—and I was one of them—supplemented these observations with such an intuitive grasp of the whole situation as cannot be described. When, as frequently happened, several of us chose to shadow the same tail, we had recourse to the drawing of straws. Now and then the winner who, as it turned out, had picked a dud, came in for considerable ribbing.

Thus we wove in and out of the animal ranks, scampering ahead or darting behind, to follow new herds when we were satisfied that the one just shadowed had given all that could be reasonably expected. As the last animals passed on their way to market, we raced home to prepare for school. The most resourceful among us dragged a rake behind the cart and thus picked up bits of hay and straw that had shaken loose from the draymen's wagons. These were added to the morning's haul to increase its bulk. The manure was then piled in the barnyard to be sold in the spring—for profit. Where could one find a better example of free enterprise and fair enterprisers?

When I arrived in America and settled in a small town in the Northwest, I soon discovered that my manure-gathering days were over; indeed, that my whole attitude toward the subject would have to be fundamentally revised.

I had heard about freedom in America. To me it had meant simply the absence of confinement, such as being tied to the bedpost when Mother had to go to the fields; and that had happened only when I was a tiny tot just learning to walk into mischief. For the rest, I had enjoyed too much freedom, scouring the countryside in search of subsistence. And confinement

I had always associated with a necessary restriction on animals. Where I lived, land was precious and grazing unknown. We had cut the grass, trimmed the vine and corn tassels, stripped the leaves from certain trees, and served our animals all their meals in bed, so to speak.

When I discovered that in America freedom is extended to cattle and horses, I was no little amazed. It took a little while to realize that the ding-dong of the cowbell was not in reality an ambulatory campanile. The cow was literally ubiquitous, and wherever she grazed, frequently not a dozen paces from the front door, she left the acrid, steaming token of gratitude. It thus became obvious that my offensive strategy was no longer necessary; so I passed to the defensive phase of operations and began to ponder the means for keeping both the cow and her generous gifts out of the parlor. Phenomenal America, I thought, as I added manure to my blessings, is there no end to your prodigality?

Well, gathering manure in Italy had been only an early dawn occupation. In that land of sunshine and scarcity there was much else that a child under ten could do, and that I did. I took sand from the shallow river bed and sold it to masons. I cut grass from wherever I dared and peddled it in bundles to draymen along the highway. I gathered fuel—anything that would burn and was otherwise useless—for sale and for our own use. There were seasonal occupations, such as cutting grapes and assisting at wine making, breaking clods of earth in the plowed field with a wooden mallet so large that it severely taxed a child's strength, and stripping leaves from the mulberry tree to feed the silkworms.

My labors in the family's bit of earth taught me very early in life the elements of agriculture: when to plant each vegetable; how to assist it to maturity; when to harvest it for the table. I learned, also, that by dividing two plots of land with a V-shaped ditch three feet wide and five feet deep, and seeding its sloping sides with clover for the animals, one could literally gain seven feet of land surface. The exacted price for such ingenuity was that the treacherous viper lurked in the shaded clover, a risk to be borne with humility befitting a frustrated peasant.

As I look back upon these experiences and contemplate them in terms of the personality they helped to mold, I realize that there were values implicit in them which at the time I did not in the least appreciate. I can trace to them now, among other things, the realization, intimately personal, that there is real dignity in human toil; that labor with the hands has real worth in terms of man's physical and spiritual well-being.

In a society where the prevailing ideal is material gain and where physical labor is studiously avoided as wholly inadequate to the realization of that ideal, my reference to the dignity of human toil may invite the charge of sentimentalism. Let me anticipate the rebuke and hasten to explain that I do not mean primarily the kind of industrialized labor which is nothing more than enslavement to a machine, work that degrades the worker and saps his vitality. That kind of labor, common and unskilled, is basic in our economy. Those who do it for us should have our sympathy and understanding, as well as an adequate reward. But my reference is to toil of another kind, to physical labor that is modestly creative and independently productive; work that activates the bones and sinews and that at the end of the day, week, or month yields something for the worker to behold as entirely his own creation. Man needs such toil for the good of his body and mind as much as he needs good food and the passionate lyricism of a Mozart; and the more he divorces himself from it, the greater will be his estrangement from life and the millions of workers who toil in his behalf.

Among the values by which I seek to live, and whose origin I can trace to my early years in Italy, is a reverent attitude toward the growth of the soil. The produce of the earth to me is sacred—sacred in a sense completely outside a theological frame of reference. I must confess that on occasion, when I am engaged in open warfare on crab grass in the strawberry patch, for example, I could be persuaded to revise my attitude toward the growth of the soil. But year in and year out, as I discover that many of the weeds are edible, the faith endures and survives the temptations that beset it. I am thrilled and easily excited by any luxuriant growth on the face of the earth, for I know that the seed beneath the clod of earth today will sustain the body or inspire a poem tomorrow.

I do not mean, certainly, that we should worship carrots and make a ritual of bread and wine, although, I suppose, there are people who do both and yet somehow miss the point. Everything that man needs for the nourishment of his body and the elevation of his soul is as sacred as himself and should be so regarded. The wheat fields and the forests, the orchards and the vineyards, directly or indirectly—these put food in our stomachs and clothes on our backs. The man who has known the need of both, he who has competed with the animals for possession of tender shoots in the spring, will have no difficulty understanding what I mean when I say that we should look upon them as sacred gifts, to be used with discretion and bequeathed unimpaired to the children of tomorrow. If one does not realize how sinful man's behavior has been toward nature's abundance, let him visit what were once the proud forests of the West.

To the hard life of my early years I attribute, also, a certain kind of resourcefulness I possess and that is seldom found in my contemporaries among middle-class Americans. I can wield a hammer, a saw, a shovel, and a saucepan with greater facility and, occasionally, with more pleasure, than I can wield a pen—a confession that must seem wholly gratuitous. I can coax from the soil anything that is latent in it. It yields to me because somehow we understand each other and I do not hesitate to approach it with ungloved hands. If friends drop in around the dinner hour, casually, with no intention of staying but for a few moments, they are soon at the table enjoying something good, because their host learned long ago how to translate steak for three into a square meal for half a dozen.

Nor will I hesitate to undertake anything within reason that can be constructed with the hands of a man. The plumber, the mason, the carpenter are men. And so am I a man, as capable as they, more so than many of them, of learning how to repair the kitchen tap, build a wall, and add a room to the house. The bulldozer has not dissipated my respect for the shovel; and the age of technology has not decreased my confidence in my own bare hands.

And I have come to believe, finally, as a result of my early experiences, that waste is a sin; or, if one prefers, that frugality is a virtue. One may take it as he will; it all depends on whether one prefers to be reminded that he is a bad man, to being told that his goodness is a trifle scant. Again, let me parry the likely thrust that I am a stuffy old moralist by immediately explaining that I am thinking of frugality partly as an end in itself, and not merely as a means for providing for the proverbial Armenians, whose starving ranks have recently been joined by so many others. Not that I am unconcerned for my starving brothers. Frugality, or the absence of waste, made a universal law, would mean abundance potentially available to everyone. And that includes the Armenians. I consider frugal habits as desirable as temperate habits in the achievement of the good life. The good things of the earth are intended for our use; when we waste them we sink below the level of the dog who buries a bone for the morrow when his belly is full. Man is potentially the most dignified animal, but he must earn by his behavior the right to that title.

To be sure, we are taught economy and thrift, and to that end, every child is provided with an appropriately symbolical little piggy bank. But the emphasized incentive for thrift is that we may gain more and more by shrewd manipulation of plus and minus, the sooner to arrive at the point where we may go in for what Thorstein Veblen called "conspicuous consumption," an academic phrase which means the degree of waste befitting a rich man. Even in the famous *Autobiography* the gospel of thrift is driven home with all the enthusiasm of a man who made it pay dividends. Speaking for myself—and I do not hope to be completely understood, since such values are so intimate that their realization must await personal discovery—I conclude with the simple statement that the avoidance of waste is necessary to my happiness and that I am disturbed by the wasteful behavior of my fellows.

I am in no sense abstemious. I do not hoard, nor am I excessively concerned about rainy days, though my habits willy-nilly in some measure provide against them. I indulge all the pleasures of the body, and within my means I live perhaps a bit lavishly. When I buy clothes for my back and food for my stomach, my first consideration is quality. If I can possibly avoid it I will not wing a lark that has lived too long, nor buy tripe taken from an ancient cow. But I do not, cannot waste. And whether it be a virtue or a vice, it is rooted, I feel certain, in the fact that I once gathered manure on the highways of the land of my birth.

II

This has been a rather elaborate introduction to what is properly the subject of this chapter. Lest it be thought that I have been led astray by Bernard Shaw, who on occasion devised a play that he might write a preface, let me hasten to explain what I have been driving at. I can state it most simply in a line borrowed from Wordsworth: "The Child is father of the Man." The experiences related above have helped to mold my personality for what it is, and added immeasurably to the joy of my life.

Three decades now separate me from the environment of my early youth, and although the same necessity no longer impels me, I continue to do many of the things I did as a child. In my spare moments I am constantly at work with my hands. I gather wood for the hearth. Fortunately, I live in an environment where an hour's drive brings me into a wilderness of conifers, alders, and maples. I have so distributed my plot of earth that I can grow flowers, vegetables, and fruit for the family's needs. The climate here is such that I can give the body to sun, wind, and rain ten months of the year. Every fall I make wine for the family dinner table and for the good friends who cross my threshold. These have learned to enjoy it as any European. They praise its quality and drain their glasses like true sons of Bacchus. If they do not make it themselves, it is because I dispense it so freely, frequently bringing it to their table when I dine with them.

I long ago abandoned the little village where I first made my home in America. In Seattle there are no cows, despite the skepticism of New Yorkers on this point, so an old problem of my childhood has reemerged to haunt me again. But a seasoned trooper is not easily discouraged. The old home town is still there, and so are the cows. I visit it frequently, and when I return there are buckets and tubs and sacks of precious barnyard manure in the trunk of the car. There are also bridle paths near my home, on which now and then, to the considerable amusement of lovely girls in gabardine riding habits, I ply my old trade with undiminished zeal.

Why, in an environment to which they seem to have so little relevance, do I continue to do the things my fathers used to do? Even on a teacher's modest salary I could sit on my fanny and keep my stomach full. Many of my contemporaries are achieving a certain spherical perfection in just that way. The reasons may be so entirely personal that others may have difficulty understanding them, but I think it may be worth the effort to set them down.

First of all, I am convinced that no one, much less one in moderate circumstances, can satisfy a cultivated palate every day of the year without a garden and a cellar of his own. A vegetable taken from the soil an hour or two before it is eaten is vastly superior to the commercial product that has frequently lain in storage for days or weeks before it gets to the dinner table. Moreover, much of the joy in eating lies in being able to satisfy the gastronomic whim of the moment. We should all be much happier if we could have the things we want to eat at the moment when the desire for them is most intense. For obvious reasons this is impossible to do consistently, even if one were wholly self-sufficient; but within the necessary limits, one who has his own garden and his own cellar has a decided advantage over his neighbor who must always rely on the merchant.

As I write this, I have a roast in the cooler. Dinner is five hours off. I am almost certain that I shall want a salad of chicory shoots with my meat, and most certainly a bottle of dry muscatel. The nearest market where I might find the vegetable, though it is not likely, is six miles away. No matter. My desire will be satisfied; for I can go to the garden for the one and to the cellar for the other. I can even postpone my final choice, for if I should incline to a vegetable other than chicory, and to claret, sherry, or Malaga rather than to muscatel, the garden and the cellar will be at hand to satisfy the whim.

There is also the problem of availability to consider in ministering to one's gastronomic needs. The dozen or so fresh herbs necessary in distinguished cookery cannot be always found on the American market. Even the indispensable parsley can rarely be found as it ought to be: fresh and crisp and full of aroma. The aristocrat of the vegetable tribe, the cardoon, so easily grown, is a meaningless name to practically all grocers. The artichoke is not frequently available. Australian kale, whose abundant calcium is as easily assimilated as that found in milk, is unknown in most parts of the country. These and a number of other vegetables, infrequently available, may be grown with a little effort and much fun almost anywhere in the United States. A good, honest bottle of wine, unless one is ready to spend a small fortune for every meal, is not to be had in a country that has much to learn about wine making. But of this, more in another chapter.

There is no more sacrilegious disrespect for Nature than plucking fruit from the tree before it is ripe. The very trees themselves resent such an affront to natural law and cling so desperately to their immature yield that it must be violently wrenched from their branches. Every European complains about the tastelessness of American fruit. And no wonder! Strawberries are picked when partially ripe that they may be sold on the preseason market, hundreds of miles away, and for three times their value. Apples are ripened in storage. Peaches are brought to market hard, green, and sometimes withered. Granted that this may be necessary in the interest of commerce; but there are ways to circumvent some of the crudities of environment. So when my neighbors go out on the lawn to admire weeping willows and to stare complacently at the barren Japanese cherry, I pluck ripe peaches and plums and blueberries grown on my own bit of earth. And if anyone should be so silly as to accuse me of lacking the esthetic sense, I shall cordially invite him to admire the peach tree in bloom, and then suggest that he return in August to complete his lesson in utilitarian esthetics.

If you like your fruit ripened on the tree, bathed with the early morning dew or warmed to its very core by the midday sun, you must grow it on your little plot of earth. If you live in a climate where that is not possible, or if you are among the unfortunate millions caged in dainty little flats, I weep for you a brother's tears of compassion while I pray for your early release from bondage. But if you have the necessary facilities and still prefer the shade of the willow to the taste of a ripe peach—well, who am I that I should intrude upon your eccentricities?

I have a further reason for gathering my own wood, making my own wine, growing my own fruit and vegetables, and doing most of the family cooking. I enjoy it. My body is still young and strong. It delights in work that brings the beaded sweat to the brow. It loves the sun and wind and rain. After several hours in the garden, the forest, or the cellar, smelling of sweat and the good earth, I take it to the shower—or it takes me, depending on your metaphysical bias—and wash it clean. Then I sit it down and give it food and drink: meat and grass, bread and wine. On the morrow it leaps from its couch and veritably shouts, "Give me work to do!"

If I were asked which I enjoy most, drinking wine or making it, growing and cooking food or eating it, I must confess that I would be on the horns of a dilemma. Such a disjunctive proposition would leave me speechless. I have achieved what I consider a happy synthesis of ends and means, a process that has been going on quietly for years below the level of awareness certainly not in obedience to a willful design.

I do not find expediency, or practicality, or the precepts of dietitians impelling motives. There are very few things I do, or refrain from doing reluctantly, for the good of my body and soul at some future date. Of course, I cross the street with the necessary prudence, and refrain from calling an uncivil civil servant a son-of-a-something or other; not, however, because I would not enjoy being a little reckless in both situations, but for the controlling reason that I want to be up and about on the morrow. But in matters most significant in life, I behave as I do because both the behavior and its result are two aspects of the same pleasure. I do my daily work, both professional and recreational, as much for the joy of it as for the value of the results it is reasonably expected to yield. Thanks to a constitution a little better than average, I am not obliged to refuse food I enjoy because its nutritional value does not measure up to specifications in the most recent dietetics. I stop eating and drinking when the pleasure of ingestion is exhausted, and not because I fear gout, or pay any attention to the sour-stomached neurotic who warned that man must leave the dinner table while still hungry. And so I continue to gather, make wine, till the soil, and cook the family dinner because, my good friends, it's a hell of a lot of fun no matter how you look at it.

I shall venture a little higher in the scale of values and urge a further reason for what the sophisticated may term my "romantic" behavior. We are living in an age when man is rapidly losing his identity. There is everywhere a pervasive feeling of insignificance. The bewildering and unassimilated discoveries in technology and the natural sciences have reduced man to the dimensions of the mathematician's conception of a point—"that which has position without size." The agrarian values by which our ancestors lived, the values of the hearth, the family, the achievement of solid, unambitious ends, are in disrepute in an age that is becoming dangerously quantitative in its fundamental orientation.

Man's daily work, that should normally be his central, absorbing interest, is too frequently boring or exhausting or both. Everything most men do is but a minute and sometimes imperceptible contribution to some very complex process. They are thus denied the necessary joy of stepping back from the workbench to admire what their hands have produced. What automobile worker, to take a random example, can point to a spot on the car that daily threatens the life of each one of us, and say: This I did myself? Even professional and semiprofessional work is becoming increasingly so specialized that it makes one rather dubious of the value and identity of his accomplishments.

I exclude, of course, as irrelevant to this thesis because of their negligible, though important number, the great creative men of genius in the arts and speculative sciences. And yet it may not be altogether impertinent to ask: What great physicist—and I use the example advisedly—will dare say that *he* created the atomic bomb?

The effect of all this upon the mood and temper of the age is unmistakable. To compensate for the loss of personal significance we have willingly submitted to the idea of quantity. Unless our accomplishments are *materially* great we feel that we have failed. While the philosophers are redefining "the quest for certainty," the practical men are exhausting their energies in the struggle for the market; and the only recreation that seems adequate after such an intense struggle is usually as violent and exhausting as the struggle itself.

There is, certainly, no easy formula for the revitalization of a corroded faith. The cozy security and the confident stride of our ancestors cannot be recaptured by a simple act of will. We must accommodate to the new world we have discovered, and if the old values are no longer adequate to give significance to our lives, we must—and, across the centuries, we surely will—evolve a new credo.

But meanwhile we must live in the world we have created, a world of acceleration, conflicts, and mass production. In this world, somehow, we must cushion, in whatever degree possible, the maddening vigor of the quantitative fallacy. Not by turning the clock back to the days of the individual artisan, nor by following the misty-eyed Utopians back to the soil. While we respond to the exacting demands of the environment, we must attempt to rediscover, during what leisure we can wrest from the struggle, the value and the quality in little things.

In the achievement of this, the experiences I have related may be instructive. The home offers numerous opportunities for creative effort if we are but willing to put flabby muscles and idle hands to work. Soon we shall learn to do with distinction, and therefore with joy, the little tasks normally delegated to hired hands. Is it not pitiful to see a man whose sedentary life is making his body a mass of pinkish blubber, call in a servant to tend his flower beds? Is it not, in a sense, a retreat from life? A lost opportunity to find real significance in little things?

I am, I must confess, stubbornly reluctant to delegate to anyone labor that my own hands can do. To be sure, my early training has conditioned me to this attitude. Except for the peculiar and exacting circumstances into which I was born, I should probably behave differently. But I cannot escape the conviction that what was once mere habit has been transmuted into volitional behavior of considerable personal significance. My home and the surrounding plot of ground reflect an attitude and a way of life; and the achievement of this harmony between myself and my dwelling has given my life a personal significance it would not otherwise possess. I have sought and found the significance latent in little things.

Now, when I sit at the dinner table with my family and my friends, I can say with justifiable pride as I tug at a well-driven cork, "This product is the fruit of mine own labor. Enjoy it without stint, for there are barrels in the cellar." And as they accept my hospitality and delight in what I have to give to them, a quiet joy comes to me as I recall the pains and pleasures of a far-distant childhood and remember with gratitude the things my fathers used to do.

4

Rooted
in the Earth

LEONARDO is one of the most noble among the surviving South Europeans who came to America at the end of the last century. He came, as did many others, to work rather than to exploit; to find the means of subsistence rather than to accumulate wealth. He fled from penury and unrewarded effort to realize, in a new environment, his dignity as a human being. He found much more than he had dared to hope for.

When he arrived in the West, in 1903, he went immediately to work as a common laborer with a street and road construction gang. For the spade of the Italian peasant he substituted the shovel of the American worker—a much lighter implement. After several years of labor, during which he learned the half-dozen words necessary to one who wields the pick and shovel, he made the appropriate response to the American environment: he got big ideas. Having decided to improve his lot, he chose a means that betrayed an unconsciously perverse respect for the "ladder of success" myth. For work *above*, he substituted work *below* the surface of the earth. He passed from grading roadbeds to digging sewer ditches.

There was a certain plausibility in the reason that inspired the change. On a scorching day in July, as he sat on a bag of cement during the lunch period, eating mammoth sandwiches of hot peppers and *romanello* cheese, he was approached by Mike, a fellow countryman and a fellow worker.

Mike was a broad-shouldered, deep-chested Neapolitan and a master with the shovel. He had also another attribute for which he was famous among all those who had ever worked with him: the tremendous power of his stare. When a woman passed by, old or young, white, black, or yellow—Mike's tolerance knew no bounds—his eyes, almost hidden by the brim of his black hat, would give her a quick appraisal. When she had passed beyond the spot where he happened to be working, he would stand upright and push the hat back from his forehead. Then, breathing heavily and dilating his nostrils like a bull, he would fix his eyes with such penetration on the lady's rear that the object of his adoration would be obliged to quicken her pace. It is rumored that the intensity of his gaze once tripped a young lady and broke her ankle.

Mike was, and still is, a sewer worker. That hot July morning he had been down in a ditch fifteen feet deep, tunneling with pick and steel bar to make connection with a fellow worker tunneling from the opposite direction. As he sat down to eat his sandwiches of fried hot peppers and *romanello* cheese, Leonardo initiated the following conversation, which I translate literally, leaving the two Italianized English words as they were spoken.

"Eh, Mike, it makes heat today."

"Yes, Lenard; it makes heat for you but not for me. Where I work it does not make heat. There it makes beautiful cool all day. You greenahorns, they make you work in the sun. I came to America in 1900. When you been here as long like me, they will give you a good jobba. In America we do not stay in one place; or we go up or we go down. I went down, but I have come up. Do I explain myself?" The next day, in order to come up, Leonardo, too, had gone down.

That was forty-five years ago, and although he is still in the sewer ditch, he has literally come up. Today, with one of his sons, he has a well-established and profitable sewer contracting business. He has put two sons through college—one of them through the Harvard medical school. But he himself, at sixty-five, with two other men, still works eight hours a day with pick, shovel, and steel bar, doing all the digging that cannot be done by mechanical means. Mike, who put the idea into his head, is one of his employees.

They argue interminably about issues totally undefined. Frequently they quarrel with verbal vehemence about the best means for laying out a simple job; but completely undriven by any master, they work like men. Day in and day out, without either straining or sacrificing verbal combats, they produce easily the work of four men picked at random on any construction gang. During the war years, when the need for workers was most urgent, I worked with them for several months. Though many years younger than either of them and something of a rough and tough character in my own right, I was happy when at the end of the day I felt that I had been able to keep up the pace they had set.

These two men, each on his way to seventy, at an age when most academics are retired for reasons of general debility, are doing the heaviest work in the category of common labor. During the spring and summer each goes home at the end of the day's labor to cultivate an acre of land—his garden. Neither does it because of necessity. The produce is consumed by the family and distributed generously to friends.

While I worked with them I observed their behavior, listened to their arguments, and frequently visited their homes. I wanted to know why they worked so hard; why they were so gay; why they gardened on such a large scale. I think I have discovered the reasons. Their behavior is partly habitual. These men were born to the soil and came from a long line of beasts of burden. They know intimately the earth on which they tread. In searching for sewer mains laid years ago, I have seen them dig and finger the soil, then vow that they were digging in the wrong spot. And they were always right. So they would move to another place where, somehow, they could tell that another digger had been before, though it might have been twenty years ago.

They grumble about the hard work and accept it with a kind of reluctant acquiescence in fate. "*Siamo nati asini e bisogna lavorare.*" We were born mules and we must therefore labor. They scorn machinery and take pride in the work of their hands: the appropriate fall in the sewer ditch, the permanence of the pipe line they have laid in it, the feeling they have that once a job is done, it is done for eternity. In everything they do is reflected the solidity and endurance of the peasant. If they ever retire, it will be to a larger plot of earth than the paltry acre they are now gardening for fun. Their measure of self-realization they can achieve only by grubbing in the soil. When that is no longer possible to them, they haven't much longer to live.

I noticed, also, that each took pride in the quality of his produce, in coaxing it out of the earth before the normal season, and in making the soil yield what no one had been able to extract from it before. When the peppers were in season each boasted about the quality of his own; and he whom an unfortunate yield obliged to defend an indifferent crop, summoned such sophistry to the task as would have done credit to any medieval philosopher.

Every summer is a contest, never defined as such but nonetheless real, to see who can bring forth the first tomatoes, the first Windsor beans, the first peas. No one ever wins, because no one will ever concede the victory. No matter who brings the first tomatoes and the first bag of Windsor beans, the other will insist that they are either hothouse produce or that they come from the Imperial Valley. The insistence is always in such verbal violence that among Americans it would certainly be a prelude to blows. With them it leads to ultimate laughter.

But above all else, they take great delight in eating what they produce in their gardens. While they argue about anything under the sun, and even about some things above the sun, they can never find reason to quarrel about this: that you can't beat what you grow in your own garden. Every day during the season, each brought bags of tomatoes and ate them as one eats apples. For dessert they would eat in common several pounds of peas or Windsor beans. And always, of course, quantities of radishes, green onions, and peppers so hot that they would blister the lips of any ordinary mortal.

Leonardo is as fine a man as I have ever known. His faults are as the unpolished surface of a precious stone. He is in no way unique among his kind except in this: that his lithe, muscular body, topped with a heavy head of gray hair, is young in appearance as well as in endurance. And that he is interested in ideas. In politics and economics he has read rather widely. Despite his age and the fact that he has had practically no formal education, the core of his philosophy is the idea of progress. In this latter attribute he differs from his contemporaries of peasant stock, but the difference only enhances his physical self, which is best expressed in his habitual environment as he wields with enviable ease and skill the tools of his trade—the pick and the shovel. As I see him sweating in the sewer ditch or turning the sod to make a bed for his hot peppers, powerful and confident in every movement, I cannot resist wondering with grave misgivings what he might be like today had he gone to college and become—what?

II

For obvious reasons, we cannot all seek the cool and invigorating atmosphere of the metropolitan sewer in order to grow old as gracefully as Leonardo. But most of us can approximate the same results by doing our own gardening. Golf, certainly, is a dubious substitute, since the course ends at the clubhouse, where there are beer, cocktails, and other temptations. By all means, let us play the game and enjoy it; but for keeping trim and close to the pulse of life, there is no better recreation than grubbing in the soil.

I have dealt in another chapter with the reasons for regarding the garden as one of the bases of the good life. Here I shall discuss mainly such factors as are necessary in making a garden thoroughly practical and enjoyable. Even on a small scale, cultivating the ground and planning the garden require considerable skill.

Assuming, and I think safely, that most of us can devote only a small space to the vegetable garden, my friend Leonardo would give the following advice: Since you cannot grow everything you need, concentrate on what is least available at the market. Plan your garden so that the maximum year-round distribution is achieved. Concentrate on as many as possible of the vegetables that must come to the kitchen crisp and fresh. I am certain he would add: Enlist the aid of the women and the children. He should know better after forty-five years in America; but that is what he would say, anyway, so I pass it on for what it's worth. Aside from the anachronistic afterthought, the advice is completely sound and reflects generations of peasant wisdom in such matters, achieved without benefit of courses in agriculture.

The ineptitude of the novitiate gardener was brought home to me during the war years, when the threat of scarcity sent many a man scurrying to the back yard to appraise his possibilities for survival. During the first good weather in the spring one might see them spading, raking, and planting. At the end of the day, the most commonly known vegetables had been planted and the rows labeled with the empty seed packets. Impaled on a stick at the end of each row, the little labels appeared to be appropriately symbolic headstones; for many of the vegetables—since most of them would be ready for harvest at about the same time—were doomed to die on the spot where they were born. The consequence for the beginning gardener was that for a brief time he had more than he could use and for the rest of the year he had little or nothing.

In planning the garden, one should determine which of the vegetables preferred by the family are infrequently available. He should next decide when each can be planted most advantageously, and then proceed accordingly. Since in a limited area one cannot grow all the produce needed, one should limit himself to such vegetables as must be fresh and crisp when brought to the kitchen, and to such others as are frequently needed in small quantities for stews, soups, and flavoring. Peas, beans, cabbage, cauliflower, corn, and beets, for example, are always available in season. They also remain fresh for a considerable time after they are taken from the garden; so it is inadvisable to grow them if others less available and more perishable, such as salad greens, must be sacrificed.

Among the vegetables that it may not be advisable to grow in quantities, there are some that should always be in the garden because they are indispensable ingredients in dishes commonly served at dinner. Vegetable soups, for example, can be prepared as often as one desires if one can step into the garden for a carrot, a bit of chard, a leaf of cabbage, a bit of celery, and whatever else may be desirable and at hand. For a clear beef or chicken broth of superb flavor, one needs, in addition to the appropriate herbs, a carrot, a small leaf of chard, and a single stalk of celery. Meat stews can be vastly improved by the addition of small bits of the appropriate vegetables. It is both impractical and uneconomical to have to rely on the grocer for these ingredients, and since they can be bought only in quantities greater than needed for the purpose, the housewife usually does without them.

The solution to this difficulty is simple. A small row of carrots planted in early spring, if reserved for the purpose here set forth, will last until the following season. A few plants of celery and chard placed in the earth in the spring, with a second planting in midsummer, will be available to the housewife the year round where the weather is not unduly severe. The same is true of leaf cabbage such as Australian curly kale, always excellent in vegetable soups.

In a temperate climate there are three planting periods: early spring, late spring, and midsummer or early fall. These natural periods of germination and growth should be so utilized that the family may have a continuous supply of vegetables and at the same time avoid concentration of supply at any one time. In my own garden there is always something fresh and green throughout the year. Some vegetables, such as lettuce and radishes, may be planted at intervals during the entire growing season; but there are others, such as cucumbers, zucchini, and endive which can be planted successfully only once during the year, except in regions such as the Imperial Valley, where the ordinary laws of nature do not seem to apply.

In early spring, as soon as the ground can be worked, one may plant onions, carrots, beets, chicory, and turnips. (I omit others, such as peas, that may be planted by those not restricted by limitations of space.) These vegetables are hardy and easily withstand the lingering cold in the early months of spring. Furthermore, onions and carrots germinate slowly and have a long maturation period. This is true also, though less so, of the beet. Chicory and turnips, if planted only for the greens, may be cut repeatedly throughout the year, will endure a mild winter, and yield precious shoots early the following spring. Beets and carrots may be planted a second time later in the spring, but even the first planting will last well into the winter. Carrots I plant in February are still edible the following February. Lettuce plants, germinated in the cold frame, and radishes, may be planted in March and at successive intervals thereafter.

In late spring, perhaps late April or early May, one may set out tomatoes, zucchini, cucumbers, and peppers. All of these plants should be germinated in the cold frame. The seed of tomatoes and peppers should be in the earth around the middle of February; cucumbers and zucchini about a month later. Both tomatoes and peppers germinate and mature slowly.

They are decidedly warm weather plants, so in the colder climates they must be protected in the cold frame until the weather is consistently warm. The same may be said of zucchini and cucumbers, except for the germination, which is fairly rapid. The seeds may be planted directly into the soil where the plant is to grow, about the middle of April. The advantage of germination in the cold frame is that one may enjoy the fruit a month or so earlier.

Midsummer and early fall plantings are the most advantageous because they will provide vegetables for the table during the bleak months between October and February. From the middle of July to August, one may plant endive, Australian kale, savoy cabbage, celery, broccoli, and chard. Endive may be planted once in July and again in late August. Toward the middle of September, turnips for the winter and early spring should be planted. All of these vegetables are sweetened and tenderized by the early fall frosts. In the temperate climate they will survive the winter unless it is unduly severe. All of them, except turnips, are transplanted. Therefore, the seeds should be sewn in the open ground from six to eight weeks before the plants are to be set out. Since celery germinates slowly, the seed should be placed in the cold frame toward the end of April.

I have omitted two vegetables little known to the home gardener—the artichoke and the cardoon. These deserve special treatment. They are both plants of Mediterranean origin introduced in America by the French and the Italians, who use them extensively in their cookery. The plants are so alike in appearance that before the flower buds appear on the artichoke it is difficult to distinguish the one from the other. The merit of the artichoke as a vegetable of rare delicacy is being increasingly recognized by Americans. The cardoon, whose leafy stalk is no less delightful to the gourmet, is virtually unknown outside the French and Italian community.

The artichoke thrives in any deep, fertile, well-drained soil, where the summers are cool and the winters mild. Its commercial production at the present time is pretty much restricted to the fog-belt region along the central California coast. Where the summers are hot and dry, the flower buds open too soon, and the edible portion becomes tough. While the best results are obtained where the summers are cool and foggy, it may be grown anywhere in the country where neither the summer nor the winter is unduly harsh. The only difference between an artichoke grown in the Pacific Northwest and one grown along the coast of central California is that the former must be harvested while it is somewhat smaller. I have found that if it is not picked until it equals in size the California product, it gets so tough and woody that it is virtually inedible. If it is harvested when about half the normal size, there is little waste and the flavor is quite superior.

For a number of reasons, every home garden where the climate is favorable should have a dozen artichoke plants. The plant is an herbaceous perennial. Each year the top dies and is renewed from the crown below the soil during the following season. This process goes on indefinitely. Each crown sends up a number of shoots, no more than three of which should be permitted to mature. The rest may be removed in the late fall or early spring and used to start new plants. The standard method of propagation is from shoots rather than seed. For best results it is advisable to start new plants from the young growth of the old about every third year.

Friends and neighbors eager to experiment with

new vegetables will appreciate a gift of a dozen or so
of the young shoots. On occasion such generosity
yields pleasant surprises. A stranger who stopped to
inquire about my artichokes left with a box of young
plants. Several days later I received from him a nice
letter and a case of tinned salmon and tuna.

The plant itself is highly productive and excep-
tionally ornamental. Shoots set out in the fall will
produce edible buds the following summer. The bud
is borne on the elongated stem that rises from the
center of the plant. The stem in turn produces subsidiary laterals, each of which bears an artichoke at
the end. The larger of these laterals produce their
own laterals. Thus from a single main stem and its
subsidiary growth one may harvest from ten to twenty
or more artichokes. The yield from a half-dozen
plants is ample for the average family.

The plant ranges in height from three to five feet.
The diameter is frequently six feet or more. Because
of these characteristics, the plants may be spaced to
form a hedge or placed here and there in the garden
where they will blend best with the general landscape.

Gardeners who have the facilities and want artichokes throughout the year will be delighted to know
that they may be successfully frozen. I experimented
with freezing last season and the results exceed expectations. The process is very simple. The outer
scales are removed, leaving their edible base attached
to the bud. The spiny ends of the remaining scales
are trimmed off on a horizontal plane, as is done with
the commercial artichoke hearts sold in jars. About
an inch of the stem is left on and peeled. The artichoke is then halved and the seed pod at the center
trimmed away. Blanching for three or four minutes
in boiling water completes the process. When thoroughly drained they may be packed in widemouthed

jars or cartons and taken to the freezer. Of all the frozen vegetables I have eaten, the artichoke retains most completely its original flavor.

It is generally conceded that the artichoke was developed from the cardoon. The latter is grown for its edible leafstalk, bunched and bleached like celery. It, too, is an herbaceous perennial which renews itself indefinitely from a permanent root crown. Unlike the artichoke, however, the best results are obtained by yearly plantings from seed. Since the edible portion is the leafstalk, the main difference between the artichoke and cardoon plant is that the stalks of the latter are longer and bare of the leafy fringe—much like the celery in this respect—from about the middle to the base. Otherwise, both in size and appearance, they are very much like the artichoke.

The seed is planted in rich, loose, deep soil early in May. When the plants are several inches high they should be thinned to four feet apart. Growth is completed toward the end of November. They are more resistant to heat and cold than the artichoke. When the plant is fully grown, the stalks are bunched and tied. They are then wrapped with straw or burlap bags from the base to within a foot of the tip end. Beginning at the root of the plant a trench is dug a foot deep and about three or four feet long. The plant is then bent gently so that the root does not break, and placed in the trench, where it is covered over with dirt to the depth of a foot or more. A foot or somewhat less of the leafy tip should remain exposed so that the plant may breathe. After about three weeks the stalks are bleached and ready for use. Thus buried they are protected from freezing and may remain in the earth for as long as three months if the soil is well drained. The alternative method of bleaching, followed in regions where there is no serious danger of freezing, is to wrap the plants securely and leave them standing. The crisp, succulent centers, eaten raw or properly cooked, are a gastronomic discovery one must not delay. And this, too, is one of the vegetables one may take from one's garden during the barren winter months.

III

There is an increasing curiosity in America about culinary herbs, and the dispensers of gastronomic hocus-pocus are out to capitalize on it. The eagerness of the young housewife to know more about these flavor ingredients is both wholesome and welcome; the wisdom of padding books on food with extended chapters on the botanical, anthropological, and literary lore that surrounds the two main herb families is doubtful. It makes pretty reading for those who like that sort of thing, but its relevance to day-by-day cookery is negligible and farfetched. Unless we maintain a certain sanity and balance in such matters, we are likely to repeat the errors of the medieval cook whose apparent aim was so to transform a food that no one might recognize it. An ancient cook is reputed to have so polluted a turnip that his master thought it was a sardine. If so, both the master and the servant should be remembered as fools. As long as the Mediterranean and Monterey Bay are alive with that fish of dubious quality, I'll take my turnip neat.

Of the thirty or so herbs that may be used in the preparation of food, the following are more or less indispensable and should be grown in every garden: rosemary, sage, thyme, *oregano*, tarragon, chives, basil, chervil, and parsley. The first six are perennials; the last three must be planted from seed every spring. Rosemary, sage, and thyme remain green the year round where the winters are mild. Parsley, too, with a little protection, such as planting it next to the house wall or covering it with a box during freezing weather, may be persuaded to live throughout the year. For these horticultural facts we must sing the praises of Nature; for without rosemary, sage, thyme, and parsley it would be impossible to rise above the primitive level in cookery. *Oregano,* tarragon, and chives renew themselves yearly from a practically indestructible root structure. Where the winters are severe, tarragon roots should be mulched.

Rosemary and sage are robust shrubs of considerable size and decorative value, so that they may be placed anywhere in the garden where they will harmonize with their surroundings. Thyme and *oregano* are perfect rockery and border plants. Any flower bed will be a proud host to basil, chervil, parsley, and chives. Tarragon should be planted close to a south wall. It is best to germinate basil seeds in a cold frame in April. When the plants are three or four inches high they may be set out in the appropriate place in the garden. Any ordinary soil is adequate for these herbs, while barnyard manure makes all of them voluptuous.

In starting an herb garden, the best policy is to procure from a nursery all the perennials listed above. If you know someone who has them in the garden, you may persuade him to give you some tarragon and *oregano* roots, since he will have much more than he needs. If he is a good Christian, he will certainly partially bury some sage and rosemary branches until they develop roots and then give them to you. Very likely he will not need to do this, since the rosemary and sage branches that touch the ground develop roots on the under side out of sheer passion for life. Contrary to a lot of bookish information about herbs, the perennials need not be renewed every three or four years. I have some plants on the old homestead that are twenty years old, and each spring the new growth is a sight to behold.

Parsley is a biennial plant of exceedingly slow germination; hence, the seeds should be placed in the ground early in February. Successive plantings are not necessary, for the more you cut parsley the more it rises to your needs. During February of the second year the parsley root sends up the shoots that are to bear the seed pod. Gradually the stem elongates and the leaves become increasingly scarce; but the process requires long enough to give the new crop time to develop sufficiently for use. During the time of its most luxuriant growth, three or four plants are enough for family use. The reason for planting more than that number is to assure an adequate supply of leaves when the plant is partially dormant during the late fall and winter months.

In addition to herbs and vegetables, every home garden should produce some of the fruit enjoyed by the family. What fruit trees one may establish in the garden must necessarily depend upon available space and adequate weather conditions. Given ample space and favorable weather, the controlling principle should be this: grow the fruit that is delectable only when ripened on the tree. In a way, of course, this is true of all fruit, but more so of some than of others. If you must choose between a peach and an apple, you should not hesitate in choosing the former; for while a storage apple is tolerable, a storage peach is revolting. The tinned peach, always packed green for commercial reasons, has the flavor of raw tripe marinated for six months in a thick syrup. Figs and strawberries, picked before their time and ripened in storage, may satisfy a sentiment, but certainly not a discriminating palate. Raspberries and blueberries picked in the sun and brought to the table, where they may float together more or less illicitly in a bowl of sweet sherry, will make you wonder why anyone would want to buy the counterfeits at the market.

There is a way, too, of conquering limitations of space. The strawberry thrives in rockeries and makes an excellent border for flower beds. Then there are the espalier fruit trees that may be planted along the four walls of the house. The smallest lot may be partially or completely fenced in with these amazingly beautiful and productive trees. Dig up the laurel and privet hedge. In their stead, set out espalier fruit trees, blueberries, and raspberries—or any other kind of berry plants that will thicken into a hedge. They will give you all the protection you need during the summer months when you lie on the lawn, and some of the blessings of life when you sit at the dinner table.

Perhaps I can best summarize what I have been driving at in this chapter by describing the arrangement and distribution of my own garden. My home is on a lot fifty-three feet wide and a hundred and twenty-five feet deep, situated on a slight hillside running east and west. Though on a slope, I have so arranged the landscaping that the terrain is completely level. This I have accomplished by cascading the lot from west to east on three different levels. For the necessary retaining walls I have used brick and concrete. The portion west of the house and adjoining the alley is a sort of a jungle plot twelve feet by fifty-three, dominated by a dogwood and a madroña that seem miraculously to spring from a common root. This space is planted in a variety of flowers and shrubs. From there we descend three feet to a second level which is all in lawn, with borders in which flowers live in decency and peace with berries, herbs, and espalier fruit trees. The lawn is on both sides of the house for the full width of the lot and extends east of the house for twenty feet. At that point we drop three and a half feet to a third level. That extends east for fifty feet to the street boundary, where there is a retaining wall of concrete five feet high, capped with brick. This level, approximately twenty-five hundred feet square, is the vegetable garden.

What it has been possible to do with this plot of earth is amazing. One must remember, of course, that it is situated in the temperate Pacific Northwest. In the vegetable garden I have, as permanent fixtures, fifty artichoke plants and a fifty-foot row of raspberries running along the northern boundary. Another row will be added along the southern boundary this fall. One row of artichokes forms a hedge at the top of the terminal eastern wall. Another is at the base of the wall that separates the lawn from the vegetable garden.

In the rest of the garden space I grow all the vegetables that five stout stomachs can consume during the entire year. In addition to this, I have sixteen blueberry bushes, three peach trees, a plum, an apple, a fig, and a pear. There are also about a hundred strawberry plants. The apple, plum, and one of the peach trees are espaliered along the south walls of the house. The other two peach trees and the fig are on the south lawn. The pear tree rises out of a hole in the concrete floor of the patio off the kitchen, also on the south side. Twelve of the sixteen blueberry bushes are in a three-foot border at the top of the wall that separates the lawn from the vegetable garden. At the foot of the blueberry bushes are numerous strawberry plants. The fruit trees and berry bushes provide the family with fruit for the whole year. What is not eaten in season is frozen or otherwise preserved for the winter. We can also give an occasional basket to our good friends.

The perennial herbs nestle in various spots along the walls of the house. The annuals brighten whatever spot I set them in. Our living room looks out upon the east lawn, the blueberries at the border, and the vegetable garden with the artichoke hedge beyond. In the spring the blueberry bushes are loaded with blossoms; in the summer with blue and purple fruit, and in the fall with brilliant-red foliage. As we see them from the spacious living room windows, we experience the double pleasure of knowing that they are pleasant to look upon and good to eat.

This may seem like a lot to produce on such a small space. And yet the ground is not crowded. Nor have we sacrificed in flowers and shrubs. There are heather, azaleas, seven rhododendrons, half a dozen lilacs, lavender, a camellia, mock orange, honeysuckle, tulips, daffodils, violets, and numerous other flowers and shrubs. The two thousand square feet of lawn are ample for the children to enjoy and to keep Father out of mischief.

The garden and the cellar add immeasurably to my enjoyment of life. They provide an exhilarating background against which I pursue my professional duties. I don't know in what degree this joy, in some ways so personal, is communicable. Nor am I certain that many of my contemporaries, with antecedents so different from my own, could ever find the same happiness in the kind of life I am writing about. On occasion I meet men whom the urgencies of war compelled to discover their own resources, and who readily confess that the discovery has been both amazing and pleasant. Now that the war is over, these men have resisted the lure of exciting and artificial pleasures; they are on the way to becoming gardeners and, perhaps, wine makers. I should like to think that these simple pleasures are potentially attractive to all of us. On second thought, I see no reason to doubt the matter at all.

This book is being written in the spring, when my agrarian ventures are in most need of attention, and during a period in the university's history when the demands on the teacher are most exacting. Somehow, the work is done. There is no time for the club, the tavern, and the movies. Probably this is a real loss. Thus far, an occasional visit to some "night spot" has failed to convince me that its habitués are having fun. Even to a partial eye, they seem too aggressive in their pursuit of joy, too determined in their laughter and their gaiety. And when the tempo lags, the master of ceremonies bounds to the middle of the floor to lead the revelers in a cheer.

As I return to my routine, I am more convinced than ever that it adds up to a gay life because every moment of it is in some way creative, and the food and drink are consistently good. The professional work is balanced and held in perspective by recreational pursuits that keep me rooted to the earth. As I pass from a colleague in the academy to a sewer worker or a farmer, the transition is imperceptible. And no offense meant either way. Each speaks a language I can understand, and what he has to say is intensely interesting to me; though I must confess that, on occasion, Mike has me stumped.

Aside from the continuous pleasure of my professional work, marred only by the grim necessity of having to grade young men and women at the end of the term, each year of my life is gladdened by three events related to the garden and the cellar: planting in the spring, reaping the harvest in the succeeding months, and making wine in the fall. The winter is a season to be endured, though not wholly devoid of joy when the cellar and the food locker are well stocked. Breaking the earth in the spring and planting the seed keeps my body young. (I know, of course, that this can't go on forever.) Eating the garden produce in the summer and throughout the year is pleasant as all hell. The bowls full of peaches, blueberries, and figs and cream in July, August, and September, bring me so close to the core of Nature that I am in some danger of becoming a mystic. The danger, however, is remote, for the fall brings me back to my senses. The making of wine binds me to my ancestors who were tough-sinewed peasants and whose feet were rooted in the earth.

5

The Cubicle
of Temperance

It was the end of October and the vintage was over. The grapes had been gathered and crushed; the juice had been fermented and put away in large oak barrels. Among them was one labeled *Vino Santo*, Holy Wine. And thereby hangs a tale of disaster, horror, and fright.

To the average American, the Easter holidays are associated with the bonnet, the lily, the egg hunt for the children, hot cross buns, sunrise services in the park, and roast ham for dinner. The merchants are currently at work trying to persuade him that gifts on Easter Sunday will be appreciated as much as on Christmas Day. When I was a lad in Tuscany, Easter Sunday meant four things to me: *vino santo, pane dolce* (sweet bread weighted with nuts and raisins), hard-boiled eggs, and breaking fast after Mass.

From time out of mind, it has been the custom in Tuscany to make a barrel of *vino santo* at every vintage time to celebrate appropriately the Resurrection Day. It is a white, sweet wine, full-bodied, of distinctive bouquet, and ranging in strength from twelve to fourteen per cent alcohol by volume. It is made with more than ordinary care from carefully selected varieties of muscat grapes.

When the grapes are gathered, the ripest and most

perfect clusters are set aside in special baskets. Each one is inspected with care, and any defective grape berry is removed. They are then brought home, where each cluster is hung on special racks in an attic room, there to ripen further and partially to dehydrate. Each day they are examined closely that all berries which show the slightest trace of mold may be removed. When the grapes are all a golden yellow and partially dry, the berries are removed from the stems, placed in shallow vats, and crushed by treading under heavy peasant feet. The must (unfermented juice of the grape) is then screened and funneled into a barrel specially constructed to withstand great pressure. The barrel is filled to within about three inches of the top. After about two weeks of preliminary fermentation, it is sealed airtight and put in its cradle about three feet off the cellar floor. The fermentation continues slowly under pressure. For about three months the barrel is watched closely several times a day. If the slightest bulge appears anywhere on its surface, a tiny release valve near the bung is partially opened to permit some of the gas to escape.

At the end of the third or fourth month the wine is racked—that is, siphoned off the lees or sediment which has collected at the bottom—the barrel is washed, and the wine is returned to it for continued fermentation. This time the barrel is filled to the top and sealed. Toward the end of March, or at the middle of April, the wine is racked a second time. In February of the second year, or when the wine is about seventeen months old, it may be bottled and will be ready for use during the Easter season. If possible, it is not bottled until the following March, or when the wine is about two and a half years old. When bottled, it is kept as long as any number of circumstances may dictate. Since every wine maker likes to cut his way through cobwebs at Easter time to fetch a bottle of *vino santo* worthy of the solemn occasion, all strive to keep at least three years ahead of consumption. But occasionally accidents intervene.

As I said, it was the end of October. Our barrel of *vino santo* had been fermenting for about a month, when father decided to go on a wild boar hunt to Sardinia. Before he left, he took me to the cellar, ushered me into the presence of the precious barrel, pointed out the safety valve, and exacted a promise that I would watch it like a hawk. Of course, I knew all about the process and had already gone to the cellar several times during the preceding two weeks to observe the behavior of this barrel that could raise hell with the whole cellar. But for that one week, while Father hunted the boar, I was to be in full charge of the cellar and responsible for arresting any subversive activities in that barrel of dynamite. The occasion demanded that I be properly invested with authority, and my father proceeded accordingly.

In the semidarkness of the wine cellar, he spoke words that still ring in my ears. "My man," he said, "I am going to Sardinia for a week that we may have meat for the table." (The expression *my man* is used by a father when he addresses a son who has passed beyond adolescence and such nonsense. I was then nine years old, but I was to be a man for a week.) "You are the oldest boy. Take care of Mother and the children. Above all else, watch this barrel." He tapped it three times very slowly with the knuckle of the second finger of the right hand. Then silence; and he tapped on it again as his eyes searched for mine. "Look at it three times a day—in the morning, at noon, and before you go to bed. If anywhere you see a little bulge, open slowly this valve until you hear a slightly hissing sound. Leave it open for about three minutes. Have you understood? Very well. Now let us drink together." And he brought to the kitchen a bottle of *vino santo* five years old.

The next day he left. As soon as he had gone I went to the cellar, lit a candle, and began my surveillance. I looked at the face of the barrel and passed my hand over its surface to make sure that no protrusion had escaped my eye. During the first three days I behaved as any detective shadowing a suspect. I sat and stared at the barrel's end until I was dead certain that the oak planks were moving toward me. Then I would go out into the light of day and presently return to continue my observation. The barrel was behaving perfectly. Now and then, to steady my nerves, I took a drink from the spigot of the barrel that held the dinner wine.

Well, it was nutting time, and since the barrel had betrayed absolutely no trace of revolt, I decided to join the children of the neighborhood on a nutting expedition to the near-by hills. It was the fifth day. Before setting out with rake and burlap bag, I went three times to the cellar to keep the promise so solemnly exacted. The nutting grounds were five miles away. I was gone ten hours. When I returned, the barrel had exploded. Its entire face next to the wall had blown away. In my excitement and eagerness to prove myself worthy of the trust reposed in me, I had apparently forgotten that the barrel is a two-faced creature and concentrated my attention on the face visible from the cellar aisle.

I went immediately to bed with a terrible bellyache. No amount or variety of medication brought relief. I drank dozens of cups of tisane, a putrid decoction of bitter herbs. All to no avail. When Father returned at the end of the week, I was still in bed and running a high fever. My success in inducing illness had been brilliant. But Father was an extraordinary man. With a kiss on the forehead and a friendly grasp of the hand, he accomplished a miracle. Had he remained away another week, I would certainly have died of a broken heart. That was the first and last barrel of wine I have ever lost.

II

There are some fairly safe generalizations that can be made about wine. So far as we know, it was the first alcoholic beverage known to man. The process of making it is relatively simple. It is the indispensable accompaniment to good food. He who successfully challenges the first two will be duly credited with superior knowledge; but anyone who attempts to confute the third is just simply a fool.

There is an old saying among Italians to the effect that when a man is past seventy he should beware a good cook and a young wife. I would like to add to that bit of wisdom by suggesting that thenceforth he should hold fast to his vintner. Forsake all else, if one must, but cling to wine unto the very end. The last weary mile should be cheerful every inch of the way, and there is no better cheer than that found in a bottle of wine at dinner. Old Noah, despite an occasional spree, lived merrily unto nine hundred and fifty years. If that seems incredible, and longer than you wish to creep upon the thorny surface of this planet, I remind you again of my grandfather who began each day with a bottle of wine and a loaf of bread, and whose life was cut short by a snake at eighty-eight.

Wine is the naturally fermented juice of the grape, with nothing added thereto and nothing subtracted therefrom. In all wine countries except America, and especially in France and Italy, the law restricts the use of the word "wine" to the product that conforms strictly to the above definition.

The making of wine is as simple as the definition. In the remainder of this chapter I shall give the recipe for a family of six, frequently augmented by a select circle of faithful friends. The recipe may be scaled up or down, depending on an indeterminate number of factors, such as the temperance and tolerance of the family, church affiliation, status (real or pretended) in the community, perhaps political affiliation, the number and gastronomic habits of friends who regularly cross the threshold. Among mine, for example, there is a stout-stomached knave who always depletes my stock by one bottle at every sitting. The doctor has recently ordered him to increase the dosage and cut down on smoking. Woe is me! Such contingencies the wine maker must be prepared to meet.

The materials for such a recipe are readily available anywhere in the United States. In such wine centers as California, New York, Ohio, Delaware, and the states along the eastern seaboard, they may be obtained as easily as cabbages and frankfurters. The minimum requirements are divisible into four main categories: the cellar, the grapes, the containers, and other miscellaneous items. Keep calm as I detail the recipe. A corner of the basement, approximately fourteen feet by seven, may be converted into an adequate cellar. The recipe for six calls for one and one-half tons of grapes, crushed regularly every fall. The containers necessary are: a two-hundred-gallon fermenting vat, one fifty-gallon, two twenty-five gallon, and two ten-gallon oak barrels for storage. In addition to these there ought to be a half-dozen five-gallon glass containers, fifty one-gallon glass jugs, and about three hundred wine bottles. Among the miscellaneous items needed are a wine press, possibly a grape crusher, corks and other stoppers, funnels, fine-mesh strainers, rubber hose for siphoning, and sulphur sticks for the treatment of storage barrels. That is all. The equipment once acquired becomes a treasured possession and may remain in the family for an indefinite number of generations. Distributed over a period of a hundred years, its cost is literally minus zero.

Wine cannot be made in the kitchen, the attic, or the bathtub. A cellar is absolutely essential. If the basement is heated, the cellar space should be walled in and insulated so that the temperature will not rise above fifty-five or sixty degrees Fahrenheit. Heat tends to make the wine grumble and fret so that it wears itself out. For reasons of its own, it does not like the light of day; so the wine cellar should be always dark. Any grape whose sugar content ranges from twenty-two to thirty percent sugar by weight is adequate for wine making. A Balling hydrometer may be used for ascertaining the exact sugar content of grapes, but that is an unnecessary precaution, since all the wine grapes distributed from America's principal vineyards are cut when the sugar content is adequate for the making of table wine.

The quality of any wine depends upon the grape used, the soil in which the vine is grown, and the prevailing climatic conditions during the period of maturation. The practical effect of these well-established enological facts is that any wine maker who does not have immediate access to a vineyard is at the complete mercy of the local grape merchant. One may ruin wine by improper care; one may never exceed the quality inherent in the grape from which it is made.

One who must buy grapes on the open market is also limited in his choice. Such exceptional wine grapes as barbera, pinot noir, semillon, and cabernet are seldom available from the grape merchant. Malaga, zinfandel, Alicante, and muscat are the California varieties most frequently found on the grape mart. The result is that every vintage is somewhat of a gamble for the amateur wine maker; but the risk is balanced by the excitement of discovering the quality of the new wine immediately after the first fermentation. It is usually good enough; occasionally it is excellent. Over a period of years during which I have crushed tons and tons of grapes, bought a thousand miles from the vineyard, I have always made a palatable wine. On occasion I have made a memorable wine. Last year's yield from a blend of California zinfandel and Alicante is superb, the finest claret, rather near a Burgundy, that I have ever made.

The finest white wine I have ever made in America I am obliged to attribute, indirectly and ironically, to a young village schoolmistress whom I met in one of my classes several years ago. For it was she who gave me the name of W. H. Myers Jr., a vineyardist in The Dalles, Oregon, on the Columbia River, a little known but excellent wine grape district. This distinguished and obliging viticulturalist has been supplying me, during the past several years, with half a ton of muscats every October. The vineyard is about sixty years old, comprises but a few acres, and is ideally situated on the rolling hills which rise off the south bank of the river. The vines are exposed to the summer sun throughout the day. Mr. Myers cuts them for me when they are thoroughly ripe and ships them so that I may crush them within thirty-six hours after they leave the vineyard.

The wine is excellent by the most exacting standards. The first vintage, now four years old, was only a scant eight per cent alcohol by volume. Ordinarily wine so weak in alcoholic content will not survive the first year, but this wine is so thoroughly sound that in its fourth year it is still intact and improving. A bottle opened at the dinner table permeates the entire room with its delicate aroma, and soon thereafter the guests are singing, sometimes literally, the praises of the wrong man. The credit goes to Mr. W. H. Myers Jr.; for behind every man who makes wine is a man responsible for its quality—the viticulturalist.

The basic equipment in wine making is the fermenting vat, the storage barrels, the wine press, the bottles and other containers. A two-hundred gallon fermenting vat is adequate for about eighteen hundred pounds of grapes, which yield from a hundred to a hundred and twenty gallons of wine. The press is necessary to extract the juice from the skins and pulp of the grapes after the free-run wine is drained off following fermentation. The juice that remains in the pulp and skins of eighteen hundred pounds of grapes will total approximately forty gallons. Without a press nearly all of that wine would be lost. Gallon jugs and other large glass containers are needed in the racking process and also for temporary storage before bottling.

III

There are three standard methods of fermentation. One may crush the grapes as they come from the vineyard and dump them, stems and all, into the fermenting vat. In about ten days, frequently less, the main fermentation will be completed and the wine may be drawn and placed in the storage barrels where it will continue to ferment slowly for about another month. Wine thus made is considered ordinary by many wine drinkers. It is characterized by a tartness and astringency due to the tannin in the skins and seeds. The stems give it a slightly bitterish taste which many consumers of wine enjoy. On the whole, given quality grapes, the wine thus fermented will be good, full-bodied, rich, and quite palatable.

Another method is to strip the grape berries from the stems, crush them, and place them in the fermenting vat to run the natural course of fermentation. Wine thus made will be finer, more gentle to the taste, and altogether free of the bitterness that characterizes wine made according to the first method. It will also reflect more fully the quality of the grape. The additional work involved in stemming the grapes is amply compensated by the results.

Either of these methods of fermentation utilizes all the convertible sugar in the grapes; consequently, when grapes somewhat low in sugar content are used the wine should be made in one of these two ways. A third method is to ferment the must alone. The grapes are crushed and immediately pressed. The extracted juice is placed in the storage barrels for fermentation. Since some of the sugar remains in the crushed substance of the grapes, this method of fermentation should be reserved for grapes very high in sugar content. Even without a Balling test one may determine whether grapes are rich in sugar. If so, they will be almost sickeningly sweet and will have scattered throughout each lug clusters in which the raisining process is well advanced. Since wine derives its color from the pigment in the skins of the grapes, all white and amber wines are fermented according to this process. These wines lack the strong flavor and astringency characteristic of red wines, since tannin and other substances found in the pulp and seeds of the grapes are not imparted to the juice during fermentation. For this reason women and novitiates in wine drinking generally prefer the white wines.

The fermentation begins about the third day after crushing when either of the first two methods is used. It should not be permitted to extend beyond ten days. During the tumultuous phase of fermentation, the carbonic gas generated pushes the pulp to the top of the vat. When this has occurred, it is necessary to push the pulp down twice daily until it is completely submerged and bathed in the juice. This provides the necessary aeration and prevents acetification of the exposed mass. The wine may be drawn any time between the eighth and tenth day after crushing. It is then screened through any strainer adequate to catch seeds and pulp that may have come through the spigot, and funneled into the storage barrels. For about three weeks the barrels should be lightly capped to permit further fermentation. During that time the barrel should be kept constantly full. At the fourth week it may be safely sealed.

The free-run wine and the press wine should be kept separate, since the latter is of inferior quality. About the middle of December the wine should be racked—siphoned off the lees—the barrel washed, re-filled, and sealed. A second racking should be done about the middle of March. In May or June it should be siphoned into large glass containers and left there securely sealed for two or three months for further clarification. It is then ready for bottling and the dinner table.

The third method of fermentation requires a somewhat longer period. The safest procedure is to place the juice in large glass containers as it comes from the press, where it should be left for twenty-four hours. During that time the heavier and useless substances shall have settled at the bottom. The must may then be siphoned off and placed in the barrels, filled to within three or four inches of the top. The barrel should then be sealed with a bubbler type bung, one fitted with a rubber tube, the free end of which is kept submerged in a pan of water. This type of seal permits the gas to escape from the barrel while it prevents the air from getting into it. During the initial convulsive fermentation, the gas will produce a constant bubbling in the water. As the fermentation subsides, the bubbling will decrease and finally cease. At that point the wine is racked, the barrel washed and refilled to the top and sealed. After two other rackings at intervals of about two months, the wine may be siphoned into large glass containers where it should be left for about three months. It is then bottled and given to the spiders for the finishing touches.

These are the standard methods of fermentation. I use all three regularly. But I have discovered through years of experimentation that a good wine may be made without the use of cooperage. All wine fermented and stored in wood has a slight taste of the barrel, a quality much desired by some connoisseurs. I have eliminated this doubtful quality by fermenting in glass and aging in glass exclusively. I make about one-third of my wine in this way every fall—and it turns out to be my very best, year in and year out. For this purpose I have a number of large glass containers where I put the must as it is pressed from the grapes, taking care not to fill them too full, so that they will not overflow during the early stages of vehement fermentation.

After about the third week I begin weekly rackings and continue them as long as an appreciable amount of sediment is visible at the bottom of the container. During all this time the stopper is lightly placed, unless the bubbler type is used. After the first two months the racking is done at intervals of four weeks until April. At that time it is siphoned into gallon jugs, sealed, and left until June for a final racking. It is bottled just before the next vintage. About Christmas time it is brought to the table, crystal clear, to inspire song and tall stories. Wine made in this way is superior to ordinary table wine sold anywhere in the country.

I am well aware of the fact that according to tradition this method is all wrong, and that the traditional method is confirmed by the discoveries of the enologist. Aging in oak barrels for the first year, or longer, improves the wine by oxidation, made possible by the absorption of oxygen through the porous oak wood. It is also possible that the extractives in the wood impart a desirable flavor to the wine. The enologist has also discovered that, after the preliminary aging in wood, the wine continues to improve in bottles through the formation of esters. If this be true, and I have no reason to doubt it, the best method for improving wine is to let it age in wood until it is absolutely clear, and then to put it in bottles for the last phase in the aging process. This is actually what I do with most of my wine. It is the more expedient way, and the results are satisfactory. But it is nevertheless true that the wine I age exclusively in glass is excellent.

For hundreds of years, the traditional method of crushing the grape has been by treading with the bare feet. Now there are mechanical crushers and stemmers operated by hand or electric motor. The passing of the traditional method is not to be entirely regretted, since the new is more efficient, and since the peasant's foot, no matter how scrupulously clean, has never been known to add any desirable quality to the wine. The beginner in wine making need not have a crusher. It may even be desirable for him to be indoctrinated in the traditional method. Or he may have a thoughtful neighbor, such as I had once, a kindly gentleman who brought me a one-quart fruit juicer when he saw the drayman deliver me two tons of grapes! A fifty-gallon barrel cut in two will provide two excellent stomping vats. The heftier children and maiden aunts with heavy bottoms will be delighted to do the treading to the accompaniment of a tarantella or lively Irish jig.

The recipe detailed above will yield about a hundred and fifty gallons of wine. As I have said, it may be scaled either up or down. One may reasonably expect from thirty-five to forty gallons of clear wine for every five hundred pounds of grapes. Since the grape season extends through September and October, the year's vintage may be fermented in several batches. In order to have wines of different quality, it is advisable to use all the methods of fermentation and as many different kinds of grapes as possible.

For bottling, I have found the ordinary green beverage bottle that takes a beer cap quite satisfactory. Before capping, the cork gasket should be rubbed with a bit of olive oil. This will keep it moist for an indefinite time. The commercial wine bottles with a plastic screw top are even better. The paper gasket should be removed from the cap and one of thin gasket rubber substituted for it. A piece of inch-and-a-quarter water pipe, with one end ground down to a razor edge, may be used to punch out the gaskets from a sheet of gasket rubber. This produces an airtight seal.

There is much mythological nonsense about aging wine. There are very few wines in America that improve after the fifth year. The enologist is not certain about all that happens during aging, nor is he certain that it is all for the good. It is an established fact that wine made from grapes distributed for home fermentation rarely improves after two or three years. Most of it will not survive that long. All the red wines are quite good after the first year. The white wines mature somewhat more slowly. My favorite muscatel cannot be persuaded to reveal its brilliance and full bouquet in less than two years. Artificial methods of clarification, such as filtering, should be avoided, since they rob the wine of much of its body. In dealing with white wines there is no substitute for patience.

We may likely never know the inner mysteries that transform the murky brew taken from the fermenting vat into the most beautiful liquid—white, red, and amber—that has ever delighted the eyes of man. I have a good friend in Portland, Oregon, Frank Pieretti The doctors long ago gave him up as a hopeless case When he was ordered to stop drinking wine, he interpreted that to mean that he should improve the quality and double the dosage, which had always been rather moderate. So he set to work to improve his methods. For some years now he has been making an excellent wine in a manner that violates some well-established principles. In a ten-gallon oak barrel he places eight gallons of must pressed from zinfandel grapes. He adds to that ten pounds of sugar. He then seals the barrel with a bubbler type bung and forgets it completely for a year. He never racks it once. The three or four inches of sediment at the bottom of the barrel, according to all the rules, should play hell with the wine. Not so! At the end of the year he draws it out, clear and full-bodied, viscous as a liqueur, and as nutty in flavor as any good sherry. Pieretti is very much alive and as generous with his produce as he is alive. Every fall, as he draws the wine from the keg to prepare the vessel for the new vintage, he adds years to a life that was scheduled to snuff out long ago.

If the reader can be persuaded to follow the recipe that has been the subject of this chapter, he will have the kind of cellar indispensable to good, honest, happy living. There will be barrels and jugs and bottles filled with the fruit of the Savior's first miracle. There will be wine for every dinner and special vintages for festive occasions. There will be bottles to welcome the unexpected guest and to brighten up the gift package at Christmas and on birthdays. Somewhere among the cobwebs will be a special flask for that unjustly maligned creature—the mother-in-law. There will always be a bottle to quicken Grandfather's imagination as he takes the little ones on his knees to relate to them the hazards and triumphs of his pioneering days.

And there will be wine for you, my good friend; wine that you have made, that reflects your care, your patience, your resourcefulness and ingenuity. You will visit your cellar frequently. You will display it to your friends and urge them to take a bottle home for the evening meal. You will take the children by the hand as you descend to work among the barrels and jugs; and as you answer their endless, eager questions, you will be giving them their first lesson in temperance without ever once mentioning the word.

They will want to suck at the siphon hose and taste whatever you taste. They will laugh and smack their lips and assure you that the wine is very good. When you leave the cellar they will insist on carrying the bottle to the dinner table. As they ascend the stairs with uncertain step, you may be tempted to take the bottle clutched in the infant arms lest it drop with a crash to the pavement. But you will resist the temptation; for it will seem fitting that your children should carry the wine to the dinner table. And as they cling tightly to the bottle, with all the elaborate care of which little ones are capable on such occasions, you may possibly glimpse a comforting symbol—the child drawing closer to the father.

There is little else that strengthens the filial bond so much as a father's patient acquiescence in the children's preoccupation with matters a little beyond their years. As they grow older, you will draw more and more upon their assistance at vintage time. At the end of the day's labor you will frequently drink together of the wine produced by your joint efforts. It will be pleasant to observe the children grow conscious of their skill and to see the pride they take in accomplishments realized under your careful tutelage. In the years ahead, the meaning of these experiences so intimately related to life will be reflected in the bond of friendship and understanding between father and son, and in the family's wholesome attitude toward alcoholic beverage. In all of these trifles may be found the significance of the cellar as an ingredient in the good life.

6

The Dissipation
of Prejudice

BUT FOR some succulent meadow larks fattened in the
wheat fields of the West, I might have married a
farmer's daughter and inherited a wheat ranch. We
were classmates in college. I had met her, appropriately, as a "worthy opponent" in an interclub debate
on the campus. When the brawl was over—an amazingly articulate chatter on installment buying, the
economics of which I do not understand to this day—
I joined the judges in conceding her the victory. I
still suspect that their decision was based on reasons
as noble as my own; for she was a blond madonna,
structurally flawless, and with a fine distribution of
weight where weight is most appreciated on the female figure. No one could have resisted her argument the moment she unfolded it as she arose from
her chair.

We had met as adversaries, but we soon became
intimate friends. Then the fatal meadow larks inter-
vened and I lost a patrimony. She had often hinted
that I might find her parents rather "different," and
that they would likely consider me somewhat
"strange," an observation which seemed to me wholly
irrelevant, since I had absolutely no designs on *them*.
Furthermore, I had just read Milton, Shelley, and
Walt Whitman, who had added to my innate inde-

pendence and filled me with the spirit of revolt. When it became rather obvious that we were behaving as if our future were to be a never-ending series of happy breakfasts together, she invited me to spend a week at the ranch in September.

I accepted eagerly, and late on a Saturday evening I arrived at what might have been my future home. Since I had been told that birds were plentiful in the wheat country, I had brought with me a slingshot, a weapon I had learned to use in Italy with uncommon accuracy. What I should have brought was a book on how to win friends and influence rich farmers, or at least an awareness of the vast gulf that separates Shelley from the opulent and insulated American rancher.

Our first breakfast together left much to be desired in the way of felicity. The food was extraordinarily good, the morning air and bucolic surroundings had given edge to the appetite, and both had inspired me to "strange" behavior. There were large eggs that had been dropped by the hens early that morning, thick slices of home-cured ham, wheat cakes made with sour cream, a pot of excellent coffee, and a variety of fruits and preserves. I went after the food as Samson had turned on the Philistines—and, I fear, with the same weapon. I took it in the nostrils; I smacked my lips; I gurgled and sighed. I took from my pocket a little flagon of liqueur and poured it into the coffee. Then I burst into poetry: "And bread I broke with you was more than bread." My blond madonna twittered and smiled as she glanced from me to her parents, as if to reassure them that such fits didn't last long. But Father and Mother were obviously unconvinced. Their strained smiles resembled nothing so much as the facial contortions some people display when in the agony of gastric disturbances. Why hadn't she told me that her parents were active prohibitionists!

When the family asked me to go to church, I told them I preferred to commune with nature; so I took my trusty slingshot and struck out across the vast expanse of wheat stubble. The landscape was alive with blackbirds and meadow larks. Ah, what a paradise! I thought of Wordsworth and his "host of golden daffodils." Old habits surged to the surface as I remembered perilous climbs in search of birds' nests, and I leveled for the kill. I had lost some skill in wielding the primitive weapon, but before midafternoon I had winged several plump larks who were so young that they hadn't yet learned to avoid immigrant lads drawn by the scent of meat.

When I had plucked, dressed, and singed them, I sauntered toward the farmhouse much excited and a little dubious. When I announced that I intended to cook them for dinner, my hosts were horrified, though they tried desperately to cling to the amenities. The father was clearly annoyed by a foreigner who killed songbirds with undisguised glee. Even my blond madonna distorted her lovely face in wrinkles of disgust. "You're not *really* going to eat them!"

What was I to say? I certainly hadn't slaughtered the plump little fellows for fun. In fact, I had never hunted in all my life just for the sport, as many Americans do. And so as I prepared the larks for the broiler, I tried to convince them that I was not insane. I told them that in Europe the swallow, the thrush, the figpecker, and other small fry are accepted as rare delicacies; that many a poor man in Italy has bought his lone pair of boots by providing the rich burgher's table with skewered sparrows. "Oh, I couldn't bear the thought of eating songbirds!"

"The hell you couldn't. The trouble with you is that

you have never had to subsist on pilchards and *polenta*. And how about the birds that *don't* sing? What of the lovely duck and the mute grouse? Haven't they as much right to life, liberty, and the pursuit of worms as the noisy bobolink? Besides, if only you would overcome your sentimental nonsense about food, you would find the lark more juicy, delicate, and full of flavor than any fowl you are so ready to kill without batting an eye." That's what I would have said had I been Hotspur.

During dinner I ate the larks, head, bones and all, with more than permissible relish, as I continued to talk what was Greek to them all. I told them that when a farmer in Italy butchers a hog, if he is fortunate enough to own one, he eats everything except the squeal. The less fortunate eat the viscera—lungs, liver, heart, intestines—and sell most of the carcass in order to clothe their children.

They were duly impressed by the account, but I could tell by the expression on their faces that they had cattle on the range, hogs in the sty, and fowl in the hen yard; that they considered my hunt of the larks sheer impertinence. I also realized that the fusion of two cultures in marriage is an undertaking for which neither the blond madonna nor I had the necessary talents. For the remainder of my visit, otherwise very pleasant, I stuck to beef and pork; but when I departed, I knew I had left forever a beautiful maiden and a wheat ranch.

On many occasions since then I have observed that Americans generally lack the sense of culinary adventure. They have not been driven by necessity, as have most foreigners, to explore the entire animal and vegetable kingdoms for edibles, a fact which necessarily limits their gastronomic experience. Because of sentiment or prejudice they will not eat certain animals.

Glandular tissue and viscera, except beef and calf liver, are consumed almost exclusively by foreigners. In the realm of leaf vegetables and greens, few Americans will venture beyond spinach and bleached head lettuce. Their prejudice against alcoholic beverages has reduced drinking to a sin and kept wine off the family dinner table. Hence, though they consume quantities of liquor, they do so at festive intervals, at the club, the tavern, or at cocktail parties.

Until my American friends disabuse themselves of sentiment and prejudice regarding food, they will not realize the full joy of the dinner hour. For reasons of economy and nutrition, as well as for reasons of taste, all food should be approached with complete impartiality. And as for alcoholic beverages, the American's whole attitude toward them needs to be drastically revised.

In many regions, blackbirds, sparrows, catbirds, robins, and larks are purely destructive and a menace to crops. People now and then complain that their cherries, raspberries, strawberries, or blueberries are entirely eaten by the birds. Garden peas and sweet peas must often be planted several times because birds have taken the seed before germination. When this is true, the offending songsters should be captured and eaten. If the law forbids it, he who hath made the law hath power to change the law. In the vast farming areas, larks, robins, and blackbirds, to mention only the more hefty among our feathered friends, are found in such profusion that they blacken the sky in flight. No one has ever estimated the damage they do to crops, but it must be appreciable. The argument that they rid the countryside of insects is no longer valid in the Atomic Age, if, indeed, it ever had any real validity. Gardeners must wage relentless war on pests that prey on their fruit and vegetables, while they are obliged to protect the pert little redbreast who eats the valuable worm and takes his dessert in the berry patch.

For hundreds of years, the Frenchman and the Italian have hunted everything that flies, and so far as I know they are no more pest-ridden than we. Furthermore, they have made the important gastronomic discovery that the figpecker, the swallow, and the lark are delectable morsels unequaled by any domestic fowl or larger game bird. If we must be sentimental, let us also be fair and humane. Why not protect the pheasant and the quail for a season now and then, while the hunter bangs away at the little fellows who for so long have been chirping and twittering in smug security on the side lines?

Of course, it will take more of them to make a meal. New hunting techniques and new weapons may have to be devised. It will take longer to prepare three dozen larks for the broiler than to truss up a pheasant or a duck for the roaster. But surely the enterprising American cannot be daunted by such trivial considerations. When, as a youngster, I needed a new pair of shoes, I took leave from school two days and went to hunt birds in the swamps five miles from home. I denuded several small trees, limed their branches, and went off to the ponds to prey on frogs. When I had caught enough frogs for the evening meal, I went back to the treacherous trees and plucked off the birds as one plucks grapes from the vine. In two days I had captured some three hundred, enough to put boots on my feet that I might resume my education, since barefoot urchins were not permitted in the schoolroom. If I remember correctly, the school supervisor bought one-third of the catch. I lost no sleep over the affair and had only one regret: that I could not afford to *eat* the fruit of my labor.

To proceed from feathered to furred creatures, what is wrong with the rabbit, wild and domestic, as meat for the table? Nutritionally, it scores a little higher than the fryer. In texture and taste many gourmets rank it above fowl. From the standpoint of economy, it is one of the least expensive meats, since rabbits multiply and mature very rapidly. If every American would eat rabbit once a week, the meat thus saved would feed millions of children in Europe and elsewhere. Why, then, is it not eaten in greater quantities?

The answer is prejudice, sentiment, and the beef habit. It looks too much like a cat. So! And what is wrong with the cat? (A young soldier who returned from one of the more desolate European theaters was surprised that in two years he had seen neither cats nor dogs!) Or it is associated with the Easter bunny, bought for Junior and later inherited by the family as a nuisance and a moral problem. On several occasions, friends who know me as something of a scavenger, have passed their fatted nuisance on to me; and I in turn have served it as chicken to other friends who were the happier for being none the wiser.

I have a neighbor who hunts rabbits regularly and never bothers to pick them up, since he and his family "never eat the stuff." In regions where the rabbit is a menace to crops there are community "rabbit drives," and the critters are buried by the thousands. What strange behavior! What sinful waste of precious meat in a world where millions are crying for a crust of bread!

I could name other animals and fishes, all full of flavor and nourishment, that the American studiously avoids because of sentiment or prejudice. But why labor the point? Let me pass on to parts of the beef, veal, lamb, and pork that Americans rarely eat. All viscera and such glandular tissue as sweetbreads are

99

rich in vitamins and minerals. Tripe can be made into an exceptional dish. Nutritionally it is an excellent food, as high in proteins as most meats, and loaded with all the necessary minerals. It also contains certain properties necessary in the prevention of anemia. It can be bought any time for about one-third the price of steaks and chops. There is so little demand for it that most of it goes into tankage and the rendering vats. Sweetbreads broiled with mushrooms and bits of sausage or bacon belong in the category of delicacies. Their nutritional value, mineral and vitamin content, are high. The same is true of kidneys, brains, and heart. Pork liver, so little used, is more rich in the essential vitamins than that of beef or calf.

Why, then, are these vital organs of the animal not generally eaten? One reason, certainly, is precisely that they are *vital*. They are associated with urine, blood, excrement, and the gastric functions of the animal. The average American clutches his hot dog and turns from them in horror. Verily, ignorance is bliss.

I learned from my father to make a rather dainty omelet with the intestines of a fryer. Of all the men I have ever known, he had the most perfect sense of the value of bread and wine. Every week end he took charge of the kitchen. On Saturday afternoon he prepared the meat, usually rabbit, less frequently fowl, for the Sunday dinner. When the choice was chicken he always dry-picked it in order to leave undisturbed the precious oils in the skin which he considered, and rightly so, the most savory part of the bird. He was never impatient or in a hurry; and when he had cleaned the chicken with that care for which he had so much talent, it was smooth and glossy as a slab of marble. He cast away nothing except the feathers, beak, crop, claws, outer skin of the feet, and the contents of the intestines and gizzard. When he had squeezed out the excrement from the intestines, he would go to the kitchen sink and, by utilizing the cascading water, turn them deftly inside out. After they had been thoroughly washed he left them overnight in a pan in slowly running water.

On Sunday morning, the woodstove was his altar and he the officiating priest. Clean-shaven, in white shirt with sleeves rolled to the elbow, he would go to the cupboard from whence he fetched his vermouth. He poured the measured drink, touched it up with *Ferro China* bitters, and gave it to his stomach, taking care to leave enough in the glass for me if I happened to be around, as of course I was. Then he would smack his lips, suck in at his mustache, and go to work on the omelet. The intestines, white as snow, were taken from the water, carefully dried, and cut into small pieces. They were then fried very slowly in a combination of butter and olive oil, with finely minced parsley, chives, thyme, a bit of lemon rind, a touch of garlic, salt, pepper, and cayenne. After a final benediction of dry muscatel, they were folded into the egg and brought to the table. A basket of crisp bread and a pot of coffee, flanked by a bottle of brandy, were added, and he then proceeded to minister to the little flock that clustered about him. I have heard many sermons, Protestant and Catholic. None has impressed me more than my father's reverent care for the food that sustains our body.

I was once discovered by some friends while in the act of cleaning the intestines of a fowl. When I told them that I was going to use them in an omelet, they were first incredulous and then mildly shocked. For their breakfast they had had, very likely, link sausage, a dubious hodge-podge encased in tougher guts than would grace my omelet. Fortunately, what people don't know, doesn't hurt them.

I do not expect my American friends to run to the poultry dealer and ask for a bag of guts. And of course they won't; for even if they could get over the horror of eating such things, they would hesitate to undertake their preparation. One can't just simply take the insides of a chicken—or of any other animal—and cast them into a frying pan as one does a cutlet. Tripe, kidneys, and sweetbreads must be prepared with special care, some skill, and with a reasonable indifference to time. And that, I suppose, must be another reason why the American housewife will not bother about them. If she has been reading the fakir's account of tripe as prepared in Caen, a process which requires eight hours and twice that number of ingredients, plus brandy and a calf's foot, I don't blame her for saying "The hell with it. I'll fry some hamburger." An excellent recipe for tripe can be assembled in thirty minutes and the dish brought to the table in less than three hours. Kidneys and sweetbreads can be prepared with distinction in about one hour.

In the realm of vegetables may be found the possibility for high nourishment and exciting flavor. The American's prejudice and habit, his lack of culinary adventure, limit him too exclusively to the more bland and innocuous members of the vegetable kingdom. Mustard and turnip greens, chard, chicory, and kale, are all vegetables that have excellent flavor and an abundance of minerals and vitamins. They are all nutritionally superior to string beans. They have the further advantage of year-round availability in the less severe climates. And yet their consumption is negligible. They are simply dismissed as food for cattle and goats. I have served these greens to my friends many times, and they have all relished them. Of course, they must be properly prepared and served with the appropriate meat.

When is the American going to learn that there are vegetable salads other than sliced tomatoes and quartered head lettuce? Endive, escarole, dandelion and chicory shoots, with a dressing of olive oil, wine vinegar, and whatever else suits one's taste, yield superb salads as counterpoints to roasted, broiled, and fried meat. Endive and escarole are available in the fall and early winter. In temperate climates chicory shoots thrive in the garden the year round. They are at their best in the early spring. Dandelion is the most de-sirable from February until it blooms. These salads are all slightly bitter and should therefore be eaten with well seasoned roasts and steaks. Those whose experience with food is rather limited may have to cultivate a taste for them. On first acquaintance, it is best to try one of them with a roast loin of pork well seasoned with fresh sage and garlic. Add thereto French bread, a bottle of red wine, potatoes that have been roasted with the meat, and bless forever the im-migrant who put you wise to the dish.

II

One summer morning several years ago, I was hav-ing an early breakfast with my three-year-old daugh-ter in a small hotel in Utah. When the waitress asked what I wished to drink, the little girl announced to the bleary-eyed salesmen and the shocked grand-mothers in the dining room that *she* would take coffee if they put a little rum in it. Since I had anticipated the possibility of frustration en route, I drew a little flask from my brief case and obliged the infant toper with a spoonful of rum in her coffee and milk. When we left the dining room, I felt certain that in the opinion of my fellow guests I hadn't scored much higher than an old soak and a corrupter of youth.

If, however, there were any wise among them, they must have seen in the incident a practical lesson in temperance. My daughter is now twelve. She still takes a teaspoonful of rum in her coffee and milk every morning. To date she has consumed approximately four thousand teaspoonfuls, or enough, say, to kill a whole circus of elephants. Occasionally, for dinner, she takes a small glass of wine after her quota of milk. It is entirely up to her. The wine is on the table. Somehow she has discovered, for no one has ever told her this, that a very small glass is the appropriate dosage for her. I have also noticed that when a certain wine is on the table she takes it with more than ordinary relish. Thus far she is a handsome creature, sound of mind and body, and betrays absolutely no trace of acute alcoholism.

She has been succeeded by a sister, now two and a half, and a brother five months old. The little brother is now in the process of indoctrination. I have begun to moisten his lips now and then with the finest wine I have. I regret to say that he doesn't seem to like it. Retarded development, no doubt; or perhaps he simply disapproves my excessive caution. I shall know more about his possibilities as a gourmet when he grows up to the full treatment.[1]

The little girl sits at my right for breakfast and dunks her toast in my coffee which, of course, is always polluted. Although she has her own cup, she prefers to share mine, since I long ago discarded the teaspoon as the standard of measurement for my

---

[1] Since these lines were written, ten months have passed and the matter is no longer in doubt. It *was* my excessive caution that he disapproved.

dosage. Her favorite dessert is Italian *biscotti* dipped in white wine. When she comes running to me in tears from some minor accident, we sip a little wine together and she forgets her pain. I am not certain that this is a wise procedure, especially since the accident rate seems to be on the increase. Furthermore, 1 don't want to risk having her grow up in the notion that wine is in the same class as Lydia E. Pinkham's Vegetable Compound. I must think the whole matter over carefully.

I have generations of empirical data on which to make some confident predictions about the alcoholic future of my children. The probabilities are overwhelming that when they are grown up they will drink daily and in moderation or not at all. (There are Italians who do not drink just as there are Americans who do not eat apple pie.) Since they are human, they may yield to an occasional indiscretion. I hope they will, since

> They say best men are moulded out of faults,
> And, for the most, become much more the better
> For being a little bad.

Their drinking will be generally limited to wine or beer taken during dinner. They will not look on drinking as an unpleasant means for arriving at pleasant ends.

There is, however, the awful possibility that the initiative in training them in the ways of temperance will pass from the home to the school, the church, and the market place. If this should come about, I shall have cause to worry; for there is no educational agency in America today fitted to teach temperance. The self-appointed arbiters of the American's liquid diet have perverted that Hellenic virtue into a Puritan vice.

Their goal is to impose upon their misguided fellows the ideal of abstinence from any drink stronger than pink tea; their achievement, to date, leaves much to be desired.

I have observed the children of many immigrants go through a curious cycle. During their early years at home they take wine with the family at dinner and thoroughly enjoy it. After they have been in school for some time they go through a period of total abstinence. The teacher of hygiene, and the coach with his training ritual, both obedient to the community's will, have taken the initiative from the parents; an easy victory, since the latter are usually semiliterate and in no position to compete with the teacher for the child's confidence. When the children leave school and take their place in the struggle for economic gain, the initiative passes again from the teacher to the man of affairs; an easy victory again, since the teacher is a dud and in no position to compete with the men of Rotary and Kiwanis for the confidence of a young man who wants to go places. At that stage in their development, the second-generation children take to drinking in a big way. Wine gives way to Bourbon, the home gives way to the tavern or the club, while the Saturday night brawl completes the Americanization I am indoctrinating my children against this fate.

Despite the repeal of prohibition and the increasing per capita consumption of liquor, the prevailing attitude toward alcoholic beverages in America is corrupted by a moral and biological perversion: that drinking is a sin and that it raises hell with the stomach. If this seems an exaggeration, why is there so little drinking in the home? Why are children so infrequently permitted to share in it? Why, when the subject is discussed in the schools, is drinking so repeatedly equated with drunkenness? Why are schoolteachers either not permitted to drink or told to hide the fact from their students if they do? Why are faculty clubs generally not equipped with bars? And does not the very recklessness with which it is indulged by many reveal a sort of desperate struggle with the devil? Is it not fair to say that these facts can be explained only on the theory that the prejudice against alcohol is deep-rooted? And that, consequently, it cannot be dissipated in a short while and without the concerted coalition of the wise who know the meaning of temperance?

The way to temperance is unambiguous, and sanctioned incontrovertibly by the experience of old and continuous civilizations. First of all, drinking must be accepted as a part of, and more or less rigidly limited to, the dinner hour. *Bread and wine* must be accepted as something more than a mere symbol. Drinking should be done primarily in the home, with the unrestricted participation of the entire family. No beverage should be consumed if it must be disguised with sugary corruptions to make it palatable. Unfortified wines or beer, depending upon the taste, the food, and perhaps, the season, should be the standard dinner beverages. The cocktail or *apéritif*—and note that I use the singular—should be taken, if at all, immediately before dinner. This regimen, and not old maids' fancies, will yield temperance. If it does not, the alternative is to make peace with the devil on his own terms.

I begin with the premise that men—and women—will drink, despite lay and clerical sermons by those who mistake a neurosis for a visitation from on High. The appropriate time to indulge is when the family gathers at the dinner table. Let each start with a cocktail, or perhaps with just a "snort" of whatever is on hand. For the children and weaker stomachs, let there be a touch of sherry or vermouth. Give them a sense of sharing in the experience, a feeling that the cocktail is a gay introduction to dinner. Let the wine flow freely. Each will soon discover his capacity.

There must be no compulsion, either positive or negative except, perhaps, when necessary to keep a glutton from going off the deep end. What will likely happen is that few will like it at first, and when they have learned to like it, they shall have learned to take it with discretion. If this sounds both heretical and fantastic to those who are still in the grip of prejudice and do their drinking at the club or at the tavern, the answer is that millions of people for hundreds of years have achieved temperance in this way. Surely, the Anglo-Saxon was not fated to be either a drunkard or a total abstainer as well as the guardian of democracy.

I do not mean, of course, that drinking with dinner is necessary in the sense that it *must* be done. Not at all. Many people are gay and enjoy every meal thoroughly without benefit of alcoholic beverages. The overwhelming majority of those who have learned to drink with their meals agree that a bottle of wine adds considerably to the enjoyment of the roast, that it brings a gaiety and good fellowship to the dinner table that no amount of coffee or tea can evoke. Father forgets the buffets of competitors; Mother finds welcome release from the day's thousand challenges to her patience; while the children, though they know it not, are assimilating an atmosphere that will help to make them good men and women.

It is also said that wine whets the appetite and aids digestion. If true, it is of interest only to those whose appetite and digestion are in any way impaired They had better go to a reputable physician of European extraction, for he will prescribe old wine as sure as hell. I once took an immigrant who could not speak English to see a physician. When the diagnosis was over and the cure prescribed, Pasquale asked me to inquire about the advisability of drinking wine. The physician said something about wine being toxic and recommended milk. On the way out of the office, Pasquale said to me: *"Quello é un fesso. Andiamo da un altro."* He is a fool. Let us go to another. We visited three doctors that day before Pasquale got scientific sanction for tapping a barrel of wine that had been set aside for just such an emergency. The first doctor consulted died six months thereafter. Pasquale is still working in a foundry at sixty-five.

It is true that taste for unfamiliar food and drink can be cultivated, as it is true that matters of taste cannot be settled by argument. Here, too, it is possible to exaggerate and to be duped by gastronomic nincompoops who write of gourmets with a sense of taste so refined that they can tell whether a fish was caught under or between the bridges, and distinguish by its superior flavor the thigh on which the partridge leans while asleep. That would seem to be sheer nonsense. But food and drink recommended by a people distinguished for their culinary achievements should be approached without prejudice and tried as often as necessary to justify a final judgment. This is especially true when the food in question is abundant, inexpensive, and has a high nutritional value. In this category belong all the meats and vegetables discussed in this chapter. Away, then, with sentiments and preconceptions! Try skewered larks—if you can get them —a dish of tripe, a dandelion salad, a bowl full of turnip greens. Try them again and again. And by all means don't forget a bottle of wine.

PART TWO

Bread and Wine
in Good Taste

For my part, I mind my belly very studiously,
and very carefully; for I look upon it, that he who
does not mind his belly will hardly mind anything else.   DR. JOHNSON

I

Further Incursions
into Heresy

It was my father's first dinner at the home of his employer, a wealthy French merchant in Marseilles —and his first experience at an aristocrat's dinner table. He was understandably nervous, for in such an environment he was uncertain of his behavior. The vermouth *apéritif* had been served and dispatched with no difficulty. Father knew well enough how to drink even in the most elegant company. Nor had the appetizers and soup posed any perplexing problem in etiquette. But when the main course was brought to the table, Father was visibly shaken. He was served an individual casserole containing a neatly quartered quail, barely visible in a sauce that immediately sought and found the nostrils of a peasant who knew his bread and wine. The issue was clear-cut: what were the permissible means, at an aristocrat's table, for getting that sauce to the stomach?

Father was a man who never compromised on food and drink. He was an enlightened peasant gourmet with a remarkable catholicity of taste and an instinctive appreciation of all that is good to eat and drink. Within the confining orbit of a peasant's means, he sought to live a humane life. Even in his work, among the peasants in Tuscany, in the vineyards of Algiers, and in the lumber camps of our own Northwest, he enjoyed the reputation of one who did even the most menial tasks with distinction. The achievement of quality was his preoccupation in everything to which he set his capable hands.

At the dinner table he was really not difficult to please. He enjoyed audibly the simplest fare so long as it had been prepared with reasonable care. Frequently he dined happily on soup, bread, cheese, and fruit; but he insisted that each of these ingredients in the evening meal be the best possible under the circumstances. He could never forgive an unsuccessful loaf of bread, for his standard of achievement completely excluded the possibility of failure in such matters. Nor, for the same reason, could he gracefully pardon Mother for an occasional slip in an otherwise faultless cuisine.

His reaction to food was always unambiguous. An excellent soup, a delicious roast, his favorite vegetable from the garden, would always lift him from a dark mood and unlock his tongue. As he drew his chair to the table, he could tell from the fragrance the quality of what he was about to eat; and when he was pleased by the promise of a good dinner, he became the most infectiously happy man that ever wielded knife and fork. His good humor, released in gaiety, tall stories, and happy banter, completely dominated the dinner hour. He was a joy to everyone who watched him as he sucked the bones and ground the more tender ones with his hard white teeth to extract the marrow. His ability to clean a bone and lick the platter clean, always performed with refinement and skill, I have never seen equaled.

His only praise of a dinner that pleased him thoroughly was implicit in the mood that it evoked and the manner in which he gave it to his stomach. Nor did he complain when the fare fell short of his exacting standards. Mother's most frequent aberrations in the kitchen were always explainable in terms of a demoniacal tendency to oversalt. She frequently confessed that when she shook the salt cellar over a dish, an evil power, bent on ruining the home, took possession of her. The consequence was that too often a good soup was ruined by too much salt. But Father was too much the gentleman to make a fuss on such occasions. When he discovered that any part of the dinner had received a reckless benediction of sodium chloride, he became a dark, threatening cloud. His swarthy complexion literally darkened, and without as much as grunting a word of disapprobation, he went to the kitchen sink, spilled the contents of his dish and, with ceremonious care, fried himself two eggs and returned to the table. No one in the family heard him utter a word until the next·dinner—which, you may be sure, was always good. Men who grumble and growl and swear when a housewife fouls up a recipe should reflect on my father's behavior and look to their manners.

Well! this peasant gourmet found himself, at the age of thirty-five and after the birth of his third of six children, in the service of M. Charbonnier of Marseilles, France. It was an employment that he had secured through his shrewd and resourceful wife and eminently suited to his temperament, his talents, and his flair for distinguished cuisine.

M. Charbonnier had extensive vineyards in Algiers. My father was employed as general supervisor of the vineyard and wine making. His duties entailed frequent visits to his employer's home in Marseilles. Immediately before the vintage he had to consult with his chief about the wines that were to be made. That involved an inventory of the Charbonnier cellar to determine the needs, and a general report on what the vineyard might be expected to yield. When the vintage was completed and the various wines were tucked away in storage cooperage, Father was again expected to cross the Mediterranean for a general report to his employer. In addition to these two visits, there were to be as many others as the competent performance of important duties made necessary.

This pleasant employment lasted from 1906 to 1911, when it was brought to an end by the Italo-Turkish war, September 29, 1911. During the five years that Father was in the service of M. Charbonnier, he lived the life of Riley. He loved his work, to which he brought unusual talents, and he came to love his employer, who was by any standards a Man. After the first year his visits to the Charbonnier residence became primarily excursions into friendship and good food. The war with Turkey called him back to Italy and soon thereafter sent him back to Africa in a corporal's uniform. But this story has to do with his initial dinner at the Charbonnier table.

What were the permissible means, at an aristocrat's table, for getting that sauce to the stomach? Father did some fast thinking. He eliminated the method of sopping it up with his bread, which he could do with extraordinary skill, because he thought that might make a bad impression on his employer and so place his new position in jeopardy. It then occurred to him that he might wait and follow safely the example of his host. But that course of action he dismissed, too, as utterly unsatisfactory. Charbonnier might be the exceptional Frenchman who did not appreciate a good sauce—or he might unduly delay the ingestion until the sauce was cold and therefore unfit to eat. What to do? A glass of Burgundy brought immediate inspiration.

"Monsieur Charbonnier," said my father, "have you ever been told how the Leaning Tower of Pisa was built?" "No," said his host, somewhat startled by a question so completely irrelevant. "Well, it isn't such a mystery as some would have us think," continued my father, visibly haunted by the fumes of the tantalizing sauce. "You know, of course, that the tower is round." As he said this, he took a piece of bread, described a complete circle in the casserole, and stuffed the bread quickly into his mouth. "Oh yes, *completely* round," he added as he repeated the gesture. "Some people can't understand why it leans on one side." He proceeded with some difficulty, as his mouth was crammed to capacity and he was trying to swallow as fast as he thought consistent with good manners. "From an engineering point of view, the explanation is simple. Any structure can be made to lean in any direction by the simple expedient of sinking the foundation a little deeper on the side where the slant is desired. For example, if I want the tower to lean toward me, I make the foundation deeper on this side," he said triumphantly as he hammered in rapid succession with a piece of bread the appropriate spot in the casserole. "If I want it to lean toward you, I dig deeper on that side." And he repeated the lively illustration.

"Once the foundation has been dug, the rest is simple. The stones are then set in place, round and round and round, always following the established contour, until the desired height is reached." By this time, several slices of bread had been consumed and there were only a few traces of sauce left in the casserole. With success within his grasp, he continued confidently. "When the desired altitude has been attained, all that remains is to superimpose a guard rail

all around, and behold! the Leaning Tower of Pisa."
The last circular swipe removed all traces of sauce
from the casserole.

M. Charbonnier, with an understanding smile and
the devil's twinkle in his eyes, looked at my father and
said, "Marvelous!" He then raised his casserole to his
lips, took the sauce in two experienced gulps, and
burst into a belly laugh that was periodically renewed
thereafter as frequently as the two men met. And that
was the beginning of a friendship that, but for the
intrusion of Italy's imperial ambitions, might have endured unto death.

Father and M. Charbonnier, in their enjoyment of
bread and wine, were typical among men imbued
with a culture in which distinguished cookery is a
basic ingredient. Their habitual behavior at the
dinner table exemplified a basic gastronomic principle: the proper attitude toward all good food is
that nourishment should be incidental to enjoyment.
Above all, their code of behavior at the dinner table
was rigidly functional and subservient to the enjoyment of food. They did not hesitate to drop the fork
and use the hands when the more primitive method of
getting food to the mouth seemed more expedient.
They knew nothing about adequate mastication as an
aid to digestion, but they chewed their bread and
meat with the gusto of men who understand that in
every gourmet there is something of the abandon observed in a well-known animal.

It is a fact, I think, which must not have escaped
the notice of those who have occasionally wandered
beyond the native village, that all people noted for
their cuisine attack food in a manner that betrays a
singular disregard for Emily Post. An undue preoccupation with such table formalities as every sorority
girl is expected to observe, on pain of expulsion from

the sacred ranks, can be expected to yield little else than frustration of salutary animal instincts. It is also unmistakable evidence of cultural immaturity, of the pitiable effort to achieve the form by forsaking the substance.

The enlightened housewife, or whoever assumes culinary responsibility in the home, will seek to encourage in the children their rather primitive expressions of appreciation for whatever pleases their palate. Insistence on good manners should always be compatible with the little ones' thorough enjoyment of the food. They will grow old soon enough; and with age they will make the easy adjustment, wherever necessary, to the stupid ways of their elders.

If a child needs to be persuaded to eat a certain food, the argument should always be that it is good rather than that some mythological character or unprincipled athlete attributes his prowess to it. If Billy doesn't like spinach, it is a challenge to the cook to make it more palatable. If that fails, there are a dozen other vegetables nutritionally as valuable. Whenever he expresses a preference, it should be satisfied and applauded. The child will soon find the balanced diet —whatever that is—if he is constantly exposed to variety both of ingredients and preparation.

My two-and-a-half-year-old daughter has discovered that the juices in the broiler, when the steak is done, are to be soaked up with bread and given to the infant stomach. So whenever meat is broiled she takes a slice of bread and haunts the broiler until the meat is removed. Then she squats on the floor and builds herself a little leaning tower. It is a joy to watch her masterful performance and to observe the increasing willingness with which she shares her gastronomic discovery with her older sister. A short time ago she amazed the family by announcing that the spaghetti sauce had lemon

In it. It had, indeed, been flavored with a bit of lemon rind! She is well on her way to becoming a good wife.

II

About ten years ago I prepared a dinner which consisted in part of broiled pork steak and turnip greens. Neither the occasion nor the food was in any way unusual, and I had completely forgotten both. Within the past six weeks, by some odd coincidence, I have been reminded of that dinner by three friends who had shared it with me. What made them remember the affair was the turnip greens. During the conversation I recalled that they had enjoyed them without reservation and that I had given them the rather simple recipe. When I asked them how many times they had had them since, each confessed that he had never eaten them again. And would I prepare the dish for them sometime soon?

Of course I would! But I wanted to know *why*, in ten years, no one of them had made the effort to cook the greens and thus satisfy a fondness for them that I knew to be genuine. The explanation they gave for such criminal negligence was not the whole truth. They insisted that they knew their limitations and so could never hope to duplicate my efforts. That was a lie; for I knew them to be resourceful and intelligent. Had they so willed, they could have so perfected the simple recipe in ten years of experimentation as to put me to shame. They also observed—and in this they were largely right—that turnip greens are not frequently found at the market.

The real reason, however, they did not mention; for very likely they were unaware of it. The truth is that they are not true gourmets. Their interest in food is superficial and inchoate; it is not ingrained in a clear realization of the significance of food and drink in the good life. They are sufficiently urbane and metropolitan to enjoy heartily a good dinner when it is served to them, but their gastronomic self has remained immature out of sheer neglect.

The enjoyment of distinguished cookery is not instinctive. Hunger is too easily satisfied by wholesome and indifferent fare, and so one accustomed to macaroni salad is under no particular temptation to rise above it unless he sets out to discover intelligently a source of joy to which he has never been exposed. The taste for much that is excellent in cuisine must be discovered and cultivated, as much so as one's taste in the arts is a matter of discovery and esthetic self-development. The difference between a gourmet and one who eats macaroni salad is precisely the difference between one who enjoys turnip greens and will bestir himself to satisfy his desire, and one who enjoys them but will do nothing about it.

Whoever is interested in the improvement of his cookery as a permanent achievement, as opposed to an occasional culinary splurge, must be ready to submit to the proper discipline. He must be ready to grub among his fellows and in the cookery books for culinary ideas. It is not difficult to get information, for people who cook well almost invariably like to talk about their methods. Once in a famous restaurant in New Orleans I made up my mind to see the chef. The manager, a smug enterpriser who lived in delusions of culinary grandeur, dismissed my request as impertinent. He was doubtless right. But a gourmet has his own peculiar delusions, too; so I made my way to the kitchen and found the chef affable and courteous. The following day we spent a pleasant hour together. Somewhat later I wrote the good man a letter and asked about certain concoctions in which I was interested. The reply was prompt, the information sought was given, and the fine chef concluded his letter by thanking me for having remembered him.

Once an idea for a dinner has been conceived, the preparation requires some careful work. On this point there is much confusion among those who have some interest in cooking. The prevailing view seems to be that the preparation of a dinner in any way out of the ordinary means hours and hours in the kitchen and "an artist's touch" in the transmutation of the ingredients. This notion, for which the precious cookery books are responsible, is as erroneous as it is widespread.

It is true, of course, that the preparation of an elab-orate dinner requires several hours in the kitchen; but such dinners are served on rare occasions, and the time spent preparing them is part of the fun. In Italian cuisine, the preparation of ravioli is considered both difficult and involved, since in addition to the filling and the sauce, one must make the paste of flour and egg, knead it as one kneads bread, and then roll it out paper thin. All of this requires time and skill, and yet, in three hours a competent cook will be ready to serve to her guests a dinner consisting of appetizers, ravioli, roast chicken, a vegetable, and dessert. A dinner more elaborate than this approximates decadence, and no decent human being should be interested in it.

The proper view of the time and care involved in day-by-day distinguished cookery may be put thus: spend little time in the kitchen, but work with care and concentration while in there. A cook who knows his way among pots and pans will seldom take more than an hour or an hour and a half to prepare the daily dinner. A novice would probably take double the time to accomplish the same results. The secret of the accomplished cook's performance is that, in addition to his manual dexterity in handling the tools of the trade, he has learned to do several things at the same time.

For a dinner of broiled sweetbreads, fresh peas, and salad, he might proceed as follows: At five o'clock the sweetbreads are put into cold water and brought to the fire for blanching. While that is going on, the basting liquid is prepared. That involves blending certain condiments and mincing a few herbs. When the liquid is ready, the sweetbreads have boiled enough to be removed from the fire and immersed in cold water. About fifteen minutes have elapsed. While the sweetbreads are cooling, the necessary ingredients for the peas are minced and placed in a saucepan with some olive oil and butter to cook slightly. While that is going on over a very slow fire, the sweetbreads are cleaned, cut in small pieces, and impaled on a skewer. At five-thirty they are placed in the broiler. As they broil, fifteen minutes on each side, the salad greens are prepared—there will be frequent interruptions for basting the sweetbreads—and placed in the cooler. Meanwhile, the ingredients for the peas have been removed from the fire and set aside. At five-forty-five the skewers are turned, the peas placed in the pan, and the cook returns to the salad. At five minutes of six he mixes a Martini, drinks one himself to make certain it is good, calls the guests to the table and joins them in a drink. He then returns to the kitchen to bring on the food.

In about the same time, perhaps a little less, may be prepared an excellent dinner of broiled pork chops, smeared with garlic and fresh sage, turnip greens in sauce, fried potatoes, celery, onions, and radishes. And that includes the time necessary for gathering the vegetables from the garden and cleaning them.

It is important to realize that in approximately one hour a good dinner can be prepared every day, and that while one is busy in the kitchen he must be dictatorial in warding off distractions. Electric stoves are as treacherous as they are useful. Some ingredients, especially herbs, neglected for a minute on the electric plate, may be completely ruined. Meat in the broiler or in the frying pan must be watched constantly.

We live in an environment that makes exacting demands on each one of us, and while many of our preoccupations may be stupid, the attempt to rebel against them may be even more so. They must be accepted as part of the blessing of twentieth-century America. The daily allotment of time one may devote to the preparation of dinner is, therefore, necessarily brief. But it need not entail the slightest sacrifice in the quality of our cookery. The failure to appreciate these facts has frightened many housewives away from culinary adventure.

As a general rule, the time to begin cooking the dinner, except for certain preliminary preparations such as washing the vegetables and preparing the ingredients, must always be determined by the hour that has been set for serving it. This is especially true when the meat is broiled, roasted, or fried. Clear soups, stews, and pot roasts may be, if absolutely necessary, prepared somewhat in advance of the dinner hour; but the safest procedure is to serve the food promptly when the cooking process is completed.

Too frequently, guests invited for dinner at seven are not served until eight or eight-thirty. While the hostess sips cocktails with the guests, the food is kept warm in the oven or abandoned on the stove to be reheated later. The roast, whether meat or fowl, shrinks and drys out, the sauce thickens and dehydrates, the volatile oils in the herbs escape, the vegetables overcook, and the whole dinner loses distinction. If the guests are to mingle and drink together for an hour, the cook should plan her dinner accordingly and remain in the kitchen as much as necessary until time to serve. In homes where a professional chef is employed, he should be told the exact time dinner is to be served; and if he is worth his hire, *he* will begin giving orders when the food is ready. If he is a cynic, and knows by experience that neither the hostess nor her guests know the difference between what is mediocre and what is first-rate, he may take justifiable delight in serving them what they deserve —especially if he knows they are in the habit of approaching the dinner table a bit too gaily and with uncertain step.

But let me return to the amateur cook who is genuinely interested in culinary self-development. His ultimate aim should be the attainment of a certain measure of originality consistently adapted to the taste of those whom he is to feed. Nothing is so well established about cookery as that there are no definitive recipes for anything. A part of the joy in cooking lies in repeated experimentation and in the occasional creation of a sound dish wholly, or in part, original. The experienced cook is interested in general culinary ideas rather than rigid recipes; and if now and then he ponders the latter, it is for the purpose of correcting them according to his taste and talents. Some of the better cookery books, and most of them in Europe, recognize this fact and offer broadly suggestive rather than binding directions. The indefinite description of the two dinners I have given above is enough to set the experienced cook on the scent to something good.

But that cannot be expected of the beginner whose

scant knowledge of cuisine is limited to meat, potatoes, and gravy. He is best advised to secure a sound, rather metropolitan, cookbook and to follow the directions somewhat slavishly at first. When the results of a recipe are served, family and friends should be encouraged to pass honest judgment. If there is general agreement that a certain ingredient is more or less obnoxious, the next time it should be omitted and perhaps another substituted in its stead. After several experiments, the original recipe will likely be considerably revised, friends and family thoroughly pleased, and the cook justifiably proud of his accomplishment.

Some time ago I gave my brood a veal dish in which anchovy paste was the predominant ingredient. It was good, but not good enough. After some discussion, initiated by the uninhibited little ones, we decided it might be better without the anchovy. Later in the week I attempted the same dish again. Leaving out the anchovy paste suggested omitting certain other ingredients, and that in turn provoked further changes. The result was that, of the original ingredients, little else than the veal remained. The dish was hailed as one of my best, and all we need to do now is find a name for it. Since we are agreed that giving dishes fancy foreign names is a silly preoccupation, we shall probably identify it simply as Veal: Second Effort.

The novice in the kitchen should not delay too long the discovery that water, no matter how good and cool and sparkling, has a rigidly limited culinary value. I have known men whose lack of enthusiasm for *aqua pura* was so uncompromising that, when compelled by necessity to drink it, they further polluted it with vinegar and thus drank an illusory wine. The skepticism I advocate toward it is somewhat more restrained. The general principle to remember is that water, by its very nature, waters everything it touches. The bulk of sauces and gravies, after the grease has been removed, should be increased, where necessary, by the addition of broth or wine, or both. When broth is not on hand, two bouillon cubes in a cup of water are an adequate substitute. Roasts should never be basted with water. They should always be bathed in their own juices, with the possible addition of an appropriate basting sauce.

Vegetables also, except for some that require an initial blanching, should be cooked in the liquid that is in them or the liquid which clings to them after they have been washed and properly drained. The most advantageously gastronomic and nutritional procedure is to cook most leaf and leguminous vegetables, such as fresh peas and string beans, directly in the desired condiment. For example, if one serves string beans with the fried chops, the meat should be removed from the pan when browned on both sides and nearly done. After most of the grease has been removed, one may mince into the pan a little onion and parsley, perhaps a bit of garlic and dill, and anything else one desires. When they are cooked briefly—not browned—over a slow fire, a cup of stock with perhaps a teaspoonful of tomato paste is added. The heat is increased until the mixture bubbles, the pan is covered, the heat reduced, and the ingredients are left to simmer for about ten minutes. Then the beans, cut as one likes, are put into the sauce, covered and, except for an occasional stirring, left until nearly done. At that stage in the process the chops are laid on top of the beans for the final minutes of cooking. Water will be used later to wash out the pan. One may readily see the possible variations on this theme.

There are two other basic principles that the apprentice in cookery should learn early in his career. One is that the butcher should be studiously cultivated; the other, that a cook has won his spurs when he has learned how to transmute simple and inexpensive ingredients into something to be enjoyed and talked about. My father put the matter a little differently. He used to say that one is not a cook until he can go somewhere from nowhere and proceed from nothing into something. But he was born in a bleak environment and knew not the peace of mind that comes with slaughtering hogs and throwing them into the Mississippi; nor the thrill of plowing under corn and wheat to keep alive the law of supply and demand.

Well, not all butchers are willing to be loved and cultivated, so the first step in this venture into diplomacy as an adjunct to cookery is to find a dispenser of meat who is responsive to decent treatment. That should not be difficult, since butchers are traditionally fat and jolly. The best approach is to compliment him generally on his fine shop. He should next be told that yesterday's steak was a dream. That may surprise him somewhat but he will believe it. The immediate result will be that today's steak will be heavenly for sure.

As you stand by the counter and listen to some undiplomatic witch—and she is by no means rare—complaining raucously about yesterday's hamburger, compliment the wielder of knives and cleavers on his humility and restraint; and when you are alone with him, grit your teeth suggestively and advise him that when she repeats the performance, that is, next time she is in the shop, he must tell her to go plumb to hell. He won't do it, but the suggestion will comfort him. When you want something a bit special, such as a top sirloin that you know must be carved out of the carcass hanging in the cooler, give up your turn until the shop is cleared of customers. And when he waits on you, excuse yourself for the trouble you are causing him. The reward will be something choice.

The second act in this drama of decency and enlightened self-interest is to let the butcher know that you are an accomplished cook and student of animal anatomy. This feat must be performed in a series of indirections and innuendoes designed to have him ask, perhaps with a smile of intimate impertinence, "Are you, by any chance, a chef?" From there on, the rest is a cinch. He asked for it and you let him have it. Suit your restraint to the occasion and describe what you have done with some of his excellent cuts. That done, your performance is over.

The situation is now reversed and you become the spectator, observing the good man's display of genuinely felt inadequacy as he seeks to cater to your needs. You want a steak? Well, what he has on hand is not good enough for you, but if you *must* have it, he will give it to you at cost. May he keep for you the next batch of sweetbreads? Won't you have a piece of marrow bone for your sauce? May he accumulate for you a mess of lamb kidneys for next week? Why, of course you would appreciate all these courtesies! And to show your appreciation, go to the cellar and fetch him a bottle of wine. But keep your decency to yourself; for if all your neighbors become as decent as you, the butcher will go mad with too much kindness.

And now I must bring the reader back to his senses with a simple confession, for I feel that my enthusiasm has been somewhat unrestrained and may lead to disappointments. The first butcher on whom I unloaded my charm listened a little dubiously—or so it appeared to me at the time. I have never been able to determine who of us two was stupid. There are people, we all know, so vague and equivocal that it is difficult to know whether they are brilliant or dull. At any rate, after I had waved my credentials before his misty, noncommittal eyes, he asked, "Are you the cook at Mike's?" The reference was to a disreputable joint in the district known among the clientele as *The Greasy Spoon.* I have learned much since then, and my present butcher has never given the slightest intimation that he suspects me of being neither decent nor a good cook.

With a friendly butcher as an associate, my father's definition of a good cook as one who proceeds from nothing into something is not so difficult to live up to as might appear to the beginner. For reasons of economy as well as taste—add nutritional considerations if you are impressed by vitamins and minerals—the daily diet should be composed of relatively inexpensive ingredients. The fillet and the tender fryer, the rib roast and the squab, will be enjoyed the more for being infrequently tasted. Exclamations of joy give place to a look of boredom and smug complacency— a deadly attitude in any context—when choice cuts alternate with choice fowl day after day. And when the children don't occasionally rave about the food they are served—a little complaining now and then is also a bit of salutary noise—they are coming dangerously close to some sort of delinquency.

Furthermore, we know by now, except possibly those who *should* know, that there is no consistency in our prosperity. So the young cook should learn how to transmute the lesser cuts into dishes of some distinction and to utilize odds and ends in the preparation of dinners that will please and nourish the entire family. A dozen lamb kidneys and a few pieces of stewing lamb, at a total cost of steak or chops for two, can be made into an excellent casserole dish for six. A half-dozen pieces of red snapper, bought for the price of one pound of choice meat, can be prepared so that the guests will rave and smack their lips. A bunch of green onions, a few herbs, a handful of spinach, a little grated cheese and six eggs, can be fused into a delicious main course for the average family. The possibilities for going somewhere from nowhere are literally unlimited. They cannot be learned, of course, by those who persist in going to the grave on meat, potatoes, and gravy.

I want to conclude this chapter with a few observations on the cocktail hour. They may seem, I fear, slightly heretical. There are two versions of this venture into sophisticated drinking: the cocktail hour that precedes dinner, and the cocktail hour *per se*. The first leads to noise at the table and the desecration of food. The second begins at four or five in the afternoon, leads nowhere, and ends alas! sometimes in chaos.

As a prelude to dinner, the cocktail is an interesting phenomenon. Despite the fact that everybody who is, or pretends to be, anybody serves drinks before dinner, the practice is not rooted in American tradition in the same way that the *apéritif* is traditional among continental Europeans. Indulged on the extensive scale prevailing at the moment, it is a fad of relatively recent origin and no more endemic to our culture than the dinner wine. It is inevitable, therefore, that in certain quarters there should be considerable uncertainty about its propriety, as well as about what and how much to serve. One can never be sure that at a given dinner party, where certain "important" guests are to be especially honored, it will be proper to serve drinks either before or after dinner. The assurance that he is "a good fellow" is not always reliable, for many a "good fellow" has been known to be strangely scrupulous about where he will take a drink. And if there is some doubt that he will take Scotch and soda, will he tolerate a bit of sherry? If he does not drink himself, what will be his attitude toward others who do? What, indeed, is proper under the circumstances?

The consequence of this general uncertainty about what and how much to serve, and whether to serve drinks at all, is that the predinner drink is in no way standardized. One can never be certain that it will be served, even where one may reasonably expect it; while where there are no scruples against it, the quantity and variety are frequently amazing. One host will dazzle the guest with an array of bottles designed to tempt even the most abstemious. With an obvious and slightly ostentatious pride in his stock, he will urge this and that drink on his guest until the latter has so drowned his modesty that he assumes the role of host himself.

Another host, somewhat more authoritarian, will come beaming from the kitchen, bearing a tray of tall glasses filled with ice and whiskey mercifully fused with water, soda, or ginger ale. Hospitable to the core and gay with several drinks, he distributes the huge glasses among his guests; then he looks around the room to make sure that no one is uncertain about what to do with the stuff. If there be any so stupid, the gay host knows how to deal with him. When the glasses are empty they are promptly refilled with such appropriate expressions as "Here, Bill, let me buy you another drink." This process continues until the group divides into little choral societies and the heavy drinkers gravitate to the source of supply in the kitchen. Meanwhile, the interest in food progressively diminishes, and when dinner is finally served, there will be gleaming glasses of iced water to accompany the roast!

The metropolitan host tends more and more to loosen up his guests with the Martini, the deadliest and most treacherous in the whole category of aperients. It is preferred by many because it is a good drink, easy to mix, and the most economical means of making a whole room full of people forget their manners. To the civilized and experienced it is a noble drink when made with quality ingredients; to all others it is a lethal weapon of self-destruction.

The cocktail party *per se* is utterly inexcusable. It is usually given in the late afternoon when good Christians should be thinking about their dinner. I have faithfully sought and completely failed to find meaning in the invitation "Will you come for cocktails on Sunday next from four to six?" A good drink, of course, is appreciated at any time, but the gastronomic reason usually given for serving one before a dinner is that it may stimulate the appetite and so put the guest in the proper mood to enjoy food. Traditionally, that has been its function, and that is why the French and the Italians call it the *apéritif*. If I could ever be prevailed upon to give a cocktail party, my sense of decency would oblige me to phrase the invitation thus: "Will you come for cocktails on Sunday next from four to six, that I may stimulate your appetite and then turn you out of the house?" Or, since there are usually trays of appetizers with the cocktails, I might decide to do it in style and put the invitation in this way: "Will you come for cocktails on Sunday next from four to six, that I may stimulate your appetite, ruin it with dainty tidbits of this and that—which you will eat surreptitiously and in quantities, for you will be hungry—and then turn you out of the house?"

I have often wondered what people do when they leave a cocktail party. I mean ordinary people who have no professional chef waiting for them at home or at the club. I know well enough what some of them do—and God bless them for their impertinence. They remain to plague the host, out of an unconscious sense of poetic justice, until he is compelled to throw them out.

These harsh words about the cocktail hour have not been intended as a prelude to passing the hat for the W.C.T.U. I have raved as a gourmet and not as a prohibitionist. A drink before dinner is sound gastronomic procedure. It may or may not stimulate the appetite. I don't particularly care. It is a safe generalization that ordinary men and women are hungry at dinnertime, so the relationship of the cocktail to the appetite is entirely irrelevant. A fine drink is good in itself, while it has the added virtue of relaxing the guests, dissipating their initial reserve, and thus putting them in the convivial mood appropriate for the dinner hour. No further justification for the predinner drink is necessary.

So the practice should be encouraged. But it should also be disciplined and humanized. This can be done most effectively by limiting the number of drinks served and seating the guests at the dinner table shortly after they arrive. It may even be advisable to serve the cocktail and the appetizers after the diners have been seated. The widespread custom of urging drinks on guests for an hour or an hour and a half before they are called to the table invites disaster. A cook who has prepared the food with care and discrimination should not see it desecrated by men and women who approach the dinner table full of noise and liquor. He should make it his responsibility to determine what the guests shall drink before, during, and after the dinner. Proportion and balance are a principle as basic in dining as in other aspects of the Good Life. To achieve them, and thus be remembered as an excellent host, one is best advised to serve one or two cocktails with the appetizers, as much wine as one cares for with the main course, and brandy or liqueur with the after-dinner coffee. When this procedure is universally followed, we shall have learned to dine as Men. Until then, we shall continue to grope our way in gastronomic adolescence and to nurse the postprandial headache.

2

The Kitchen
and the Soup Kettle

MIKE, MY companion on the sewer gang, was wont to divide all human beings into two categories: Christians and barbarians. His classifications were rigidly objective, for they were made sight unseen and without reference to the subject's standing in the community. As we drove from one corner of the city to the next, intent upon channeling our fellow citizen's excrement to the sea, Mike carefully appraised each garden. Where he saw one where vegetables predominated over flowers, he repeated his intuitive formula: *"Eh, qui ci sta un cristiano!"* Ah, a Christian lives here! At the last count the barbarians were out in front a hundred to one.

Mike's formula may be applied in a different though related context. A survey of any kitchen will reveal whether it is presided over by a cook or a mere dispenser of "wholesome food." Where the kitchen pantry is well stocked and the kitchen utensils are adequate, one may confidently exclaim, "Ah, a cook lives here." For it is easier to build a house without square and saw than to cook a good dinner without adequate utensils and culinary aids.

During the past fifteen years I have been frequently asked by friends, and occasionally by friends of friends, to do the cooking for certain special occasions. I don't remember a single instance when I have not been frustrated by lack of appropriate utensils and such culinary accessories as bouillon cubes and tinned broth. The last time I served as a friendly peripatetic chef, I was asked to prepare spaghetti for twenty guests. When I made my way into the kitchen, laden with five pounds of spaghetti and other necessary ingredients, I discovered that the largest kettle in the house was a three-quart pot, scarcely large enough to hold one of the five pounds. There wasn't even a dishpan that might be used as a substitute! The guests were hungry and their expectations were high, so I had to do the best possible with the available tools.

I gathered the four largest pans in the house. They were adequate for about half the spaghetti. It is axiomatic in spaghetti cookery that the paste must boil freely and loosely in plenty of water so that the surface covering of starch may be washed away. Where this is not done, the result is a thick, sticky, starchy mess that no amount of sauce can redeem. And that is what I was obliged to serve. The guests liked it and praised it highly. I thought it was awful and held my peace.

So before we begin boiling and simmering and broiling, we had better agree on certain minimum requirements by way of pots and pans and kitchen accessories in general. Since our immediate concern is with soups, we may prescribe as our first utensil on the list the one that is most frequently used for that purpose. It should be a kettle of two- or three-gallon capacity. Life is a long time and the future uncertain, so let us make it a durable pot, one that may be handed down from generation to generation, and used, when the occasion requires it, for the infant gourmet's bath. It will also be useful for boiling spaghetti, blanching vegetables for the cold storage locker, and sterilizing jars during the canning season.

In every kitchen there should also be a fine-mesh strainer, one that will hold back tomato seeds and other small particles. It should be about eight inches in diameter. The resourceful housewife will find a hundred uses for it from day to day. I use mine every fall for straining the wine as it comes from the press or the fermenting vat.

Since the turkey is our traditional festive bird, nearly every household has an adequate roaster. Those who have not yet acquired it should select one of heavy metal, with a flat bottom and a close-fitting lid. It may be frequently used for meat, fowl, and fish dishes whose distinctive character is achieved through simmering in appropriate sauces. If the roaster on hand is not adequate for this purpose (and it won't be unless it has a flat bottom) then a spacious skillet-type pan of cast aluminum or other heavy metal must be procured. It should be about twelve inches in diameter, four inches or more deep, and provided with a tight-fitting lid. Ample space is needed so that when meat is simmered in a sauce, each piece will be immersed in it as it rests on the bottom of the pan. A skillet of the size here suggested is adequate for cooking about six pounds of chicken or other meat. For a small family group, a smaller skillet of the same general type should supplement the larger one which will be reserved for guest dinners.

Such skillets may also be used for frying; so where these are stocked in the kitchen, the ordinary large frying pan may be dispensed with. But a smaller frying pan of heavy metal, and also equipped with a close-fitting lid, is indispensable. Its various uses will readily suggest themselves to anyone who takes his cooking seriously.

Adequate saucepans are as necessary as they are

seldom found in the average kitchen. One will do, but two will be more convenient. Three will be unmistakable evidence that the housewife is a Christian— and a cook. They, too, should be bought with the grandchildren in mind. The best are heavy and flat-bottomed, pans that will take the heat without cringing and hold it in leash. The offspring of sons and daughters, proud beneficiaries of their ancestors' sweated accumulations, will display them in the next century as the pans that made Grandmother a model wife. They may even boast, with a slight touch of culinary decadence, that they have improved with age.

These saucepans, in various sizes, must be immediately stocked. They will be used for the simmering of sauces and more frequently for other purposes. Fresh vegetables, such as peas, string beans, and carrots, will cook to perfection in their appropriate condiments in such pans. They may also be used for the daintier soups, such as mushroom, cream of tomato, or clear broth, taken from the week's supply made in the master kettle. And where else can one sterilize so efficiently and appropriately the nipples for baby's bottle than in one of these sturdy saucepans? Let Escoffier scoff if he will.

A broiling tray and rack and several eight-inch skewers of stainless steel are as necessary as the stove. Earthenware casseroles are nice to have, but as they are primarily intended for use on the wood range and crack easily on the concentrated heat of electricity or gas, they are a pretty adornment from a more primitive kitchen and quite unsuited to our own. I omit also from this list the more obvious utensils which are found in nearly every kitchen.

He who would cook well must first learn to mince. The apprentice mason carries bricks and mortar; the apprentice cook wields the mincing knife and cleaver.

Where you find in the kitchen a light cleaver, a heavy knife with a straight, sharp edge, and a spacious mincing board of hard wood, you may be certain that you are in the home of a chef. The gastronomic adolescent would insist on mortar and pestle, but these are tools of primitive man and the apothecary's symbol. The mincing board and the sharp knife or cleaver, in skilled hands, will reduce to a pulp anything that requires such treatment. Whatever the means employed, the important thing to realize is that mincing is to cooking what H2 is to water. Let the good cook devise his own means. But mince he must. If he is wise, he will take an old trooper's advice and procure immediately the implements here suggested.

There is not a cookbook worth the paper on which it is printed which does not suggest the frequent use of two famous Italian cheeses: *Parmigiano* and *Romano*. They are hard and dry and full of flavor, the classic grating cheeses in occidental cookery. The dairy interests have recently cluttered the market with "Parmesan type" counterfeits that aren't worth a damn. They are so foul that they may safely be guaranteed to ruin any food on which they are sprinkled. Nor is it safe to buy the grated product even in a reputable Italian store; for the temptation is too great to grind up all the dry and stale odds and ends of cheese that cannot otherwise be disposed of, and palm them off as grated Parmigiano. The prudent cook will buy a chunk of the genuine cheese and grate it in the kitchen as needed.

In describing a particularly affectionate relationship, the Italians say, "*Siamo amici come il pane e il formaggio.*" We are as intimate as bread and cheese. And that aptly expresses their predilection for cheese as an accompaniment to bread. Wine, of course, is taken for granted as the appropriate beverage. And the cheeses they most frequently eat with their bread are *Parmigiano, Romano* and *Pecorino,* the latter being a sharp goat's milk cheese somewhat akin to *Romano.* A thick slice of crisp French bread, a thin slice of one of these cheeses, and a glass of wine, is still the luncheon that binds me close to my ancestors.

Herbs, condiments, and certain basic staples are found in all kitchens where superior food is habitually served. The basic culinary herbs, such as basil, rosemary, sage, bay leaf, *oregano,* thyme, and tarragon are now available in dry or powdered form in the better groceries. With the exception of bay leaf, none of these dry herbs is an adequate substitute for the fresh product. The flavor of the aromatic plants is in the volatile oils in the leaf. In the drying process, the aroma is either partially dissipated or metamorphosed into something akin to, but different from, the fragrance characteristic of the green plants. Dry sage and rosemary are so transformed as to be practically useless. *Oregano,* used so much by southern Italians in salads, has a strong medicinal flavor quite unlike that of the green leaves. I use the fresh *oregano* regularly, but I have been unable to cultivate a taste for the dry. Basil, if dried slowly and stored in sealed containers, retains much of its original aroma. The commercial product, however, is not very satisfactory; so the cook should grow and dry his own. Dry tarragon leaves are quite satisfactory in the preparation of fish sauces.

Fortunately, all of these herbs except basil are hardy perennials and may be had fresh throughout the year in the milder climates, if the cook will take the trouble to grow them in the garden. Tarragon is dormant during the winter months; but sage, rosemary, *oregano,* and thyme, with some protection, will remain green the full twelve months and bloom into full luxuriance during the spring and summer. So I cannot honestly recommend more dry herbs for the kitchen than bay leaf, basil, and tarragon. Where the fresh are available, no one would want to use the dry; but where they are not easily obtainable, there is really no cause for despair, since nearly all fish, flesh, and fowl, as well as many sauces, may be given an excellent flavor with parsley, celery, onion, and garlic —all of them stock commodities in any grocery. During moments of faith and credulity I am almost tempted to believe that what is most necessary in the preparation of distinguished food was preordained to grow with savage fury and to withstand all weather. This is certainly true of rosemary, sage, and thyme; it is even more true of onion, garlic, parsley, and celery. They are the most ubiquitous and indispensable flavors. Give me these every day of the year and you will want to come again for dinner. Temperamentally as well as intellectually I dislike imperatives, but this one I insist upon and live faithfully by: No cook should ever be without garlic, parsley, onion, and celery. I have listed them in the order of absolute necessity.

In insisting upon these basic aromatics, I do not mean to discourage experimentation with other herbs. I have a dozen or so in my garden and I have tried them all. The results have not been wholly gratifying. The use of less familiar herbs, such as balm, anise, burnet, borage, fennel, and mint, is so limited in cookery that they may well be left to the amateur and the professional herbalist. They are used mainly in salads and beverages designed for people who enjoy novelty more than good food. The current interest in herbs is so exploited by the magazines and some cookery books that there is danger of confusion on the whole subject. So my best advice to anyone interested in improving his cuisine is that he should concentrate on the herbs I have suggested, in as many combinations as he can devise and which prove satisfactory. When to them are added capers and chives, there is enough latent variety to satisfy all but the most jaded palate.

Garlic is a recent discovery in American cuisine, so the books on cookery give it some clever play and special attention. What it deserves is more attention and less clever play. The human body, when it freezes into eternal silence, is said to be worth about ninety-eight cents.[1] The body of an ordinary south European, if we could devise the means for extracting the garlic from it, would be worth a bushel of gold.

The Greeks were the first great metaphysicians. They sought to discover the first principles of Being, to answer the question: What is real? One of their answers was that all body is ultimately composed of four elements: earth, air, fire, and water. They were four-fifths right. Like so many great scholars after them, they had the complete answer within their grasp but couldn't quite cut the mustard and so left the puzzle to later generations. Garlic, of course, is the fifth element. It is one of the major ironies of life that the Greeks, of all people, should have fallen so short of the Truth.

I once worked with a powerful son of Athens whose reverence for garlic left nothing to be desired. He used it daily internally and externally. He ate it regularly raw and rubbed it on his chest and in his nostrils. He was a dynamo of flesh and bones who visited physicians only to be admired and to give them a little advice. Once he invited me to his bachelor's hovel for dinner. This was the menu: two chickens roasted with

[1] Inflation has reached into the grave. The new list price is much, much higher.

garlic and rosemary, two loaves of French bread, each cut lengthwise and smeared with garlic and olive oil, two heads of raw garlic (about twenty cloves), two quarts of wine, and two enormous raw chicory roots. The garlic in such a man's body, I surmise, must be worth a fortune.

Well, this embodiment of the Socratic virtues and I worked in a stuffy freight car, loading fir doors for all parts of the world. We were always at close quarters, never more than two paces apart. His powerful breath, pungent and sharp as the most corroding acid, kept my body in a permanently aseptic state. As it mingled and fused with the anomalous stench of freight cars, my devotion to garlic was severely taxed. But never really shaken. My final, considered judgment is that the hardy bulb blesses and ennobles everything it touches—with the possible exception of ice cream and pie. On meats, in sauces, in the preparation of most vegetables, it is almost impossible to use it too recklessly. The vegetable soup, served with buttered toast rubbed generously with garlic, becomes a veritable feast. Three or four cloves fried with the potatoes produce tantalizing results.

The possibilities are without limit; but, I repeat, it must be used with a certain abandon. The American's attitude toward garlic is a trifle coy, and reflects a basic uncertainty about its use and its propriety. This is revealed in such culinary advice as: "Rub the salad bowl lightly with garlic—remember, a little goes a long, long way, *etc.* When using it in frying meat, impale a clove on a toothpick, perhaps with a little red banner tied on the end of it, so that at the proper time the odious bulb may be identified, removed, and thrown away."

This is all wrong, and it betrays an undue preoccupation with the social consequences of using garlic in cookery. The salad bowl should be rubbed *thoroughly*, and the garlic should be scraped with a sharp knife on both surfaces of the steak that is to be broiled or fried. One either uses garlic or one does not. There is no happy compromise. Let him who is so disposed worry about the social consequences of his indulgence.

Capers and mushrooms are necessary in good cookery. The former, flower buds of a Mediterranean shrub, are used extensively in French and Italian cookery. They are too frequently preserved in vinegar, and that is a pity, for the acetic acid destroys their flavor. They are also to be found, now and then, dried in salt. Get them that way if you can, for that preserves their flavor best. If mushrooms cannot be obtained fresh, they are better dried than tinned when used as ingredients in sauces. As a matter of fact, the flavor of some dried mushrooms, such as the fairy ring, is superior to that of the fresh. This diminutive mushroom grows in such profusion on lawns and golf courses that in a single afternoon, any time during the spring or fall, I can gather a year's supply.

Among the spices, the most important are black and cayenne pepper, nutmeg, and allspice. Stock others too, but these are basic. Bouillon cubes and tinned broth should always be on hand. So should tomatoes, tomato paste, tinned sea food, Worcestershire and Tabasco sauce. And, of course, wine, both white and red. Such staples as paste and legumes are stock requirements. Add to these ham, salt pork, salami, and you will always be ready for the unexpected guest who has scented your reputation. With a kitchen thus equipped, flanked by a garden and a wine cellar, we are ready to go to work. And soup is appropriately our first concern.

II

There are, I know, dozens and dozens of soups. One so disposed might write a volume about them. Since I am more interested in improving our daily dinner than in culinary lore, I shall set limits to my discussion in harmony with this excusable preoccupation. I also feel that it is unnecessary to repeat well-known recipes or such as are to be found in all the cookbooks. So I shall emphasize two main categories of soup: those that are most adequate as an introduction to dinner, and those that are most satisfactory as meals in themselves.

With all due reverence for such soups as onion, cream of tomato, cream of mushroom, and their various kin, I proceed confidently to the generalization that a good broth is the best and most appropriate introduction to a fine dinner. The three kinds of broth I prefer are beef, chicken, and a combination of the two. And this is the way to make them.

For beef broth, place in the master kettle four or five quarts of water, one oxtail, one knucklebone or soupbone, a piece of shinbone with meat attached, and two pounds of beef short ribs. Trim away as much of the fat as you can. When the broth comes to a boil, reduce the heat and let the soup simmer with the kettle partially covered. It should cook about three hours. On the theory that searing or quick immersion in boiling water seals in the juices of the meat, some advise starting the soup in cold water. I have found by experience that it makes no perceptible difference and I am ready to perform the blindfold test on anybody who disagrees. So proceed as best suits your temperament.

During the simmering, the soup should be skimmed

and the liquefied fat removed as often as is necessary. The following seasoning is added about three-quarters of an hour before the cooking is completed: salt, a few peppercorns, a small carrot, a small onion, a stalk of celery with the leaves, three or four large sprigs of parsley, and a large ripe tomato or a cup of tinned tomatoes. Some would add a bay leaf and three or four cloves, while others would leave out the tomato. Let each suit his own taste. If a greater quantity of broth is desired increase all the ingredients accordingly.

The exquisite broth that results may be used in various ways. And how about the precious meat? There is only one sensible answer—eat it as the basis for a boiled dinner on the day the broth is made. Cook separately as many vegetables as you desire and serve them with the meat hot from the kettle. Dill pickles, horse radish or mustard, a bottle of wine, and good bread will bring the dinner to life. When the broth has cooled, store it in the refrigerator and later lift off the fat that has solidified on top.

For chicken broth, cut in quarters a stewing hen and proceed according to the above recipe, omitting the tomato. Use about a quart of water to one and one-half pounds of chicken. For chicken and beef combined, add half a stewing hen to the above quantity of meat, increase the water accordingly, and add the seasoning listed for beef broth. It is important to remember that the herbs and vegetables are added to the broth as seasoning; so they should be used sparingly. The practice of adding a lot of vegetables to the meat, while it may produce a nutritious soup, destroys the characteristic flavor of the broth.

Clear broth and its derivatives are intended mainly as a first course in the dinner; so they should be prepared to whet the appetite and served in small quantities. With clear broth as a base, an imaginative cook may prepare any number of light delectable soups. Whatever is added should heighten rather than impair the flavor of the broth. I offer the following suggestions: A small dish of clear broth, with perhaps a dash of minced parsley and minced lemon rind, topped with a teaspoon of grated *Parmigiano*, is first in the order of preference. For variety, a spoonful or two of dry sherry may be added to each serving. That is an adornment that I wouldn't indulge too frequently, but if you like it, it will do you no harm. A good cook knows when to leave well enough alone.

My next choice would be broth with a bit of escarole or the outer leaves of plain lettuce. The leaves are first blanched, then drained and cut coarsely. They are then thrown into the boiling broth for the final minutes of cooking. A heaping tablespoonful for each serving is plenty. The escarole may be cooked directly into the broth if one does not object—as he should—to the pronounced bitter taste which will result. When served, let each guest scatter over his portion a teaspoonful of grated cheese.

A third variation on this theme is broth and a bit of rice, or some very fine paste such as *capellini*. If rice is used, allow half a tablespoonful, raw, for each serving and precook it in plain water until about three-fourths done. Then finish the cooking in the boiling broth. The paste, about a cupful for six servings, need not be precooked. Serve with grated cheese and minced parsley.

A slightly heavier but excellent soup may be made in the following manner: For six servings, beat an egg and half a cup of grated cheese. Add to the boiling broth and cook for about a minute or two, stirring briskly all the while. Color each dish with a pinch of finely minced chervil—fresh from the garden, of course. Cheese on this dish would be slightly re﹐ dundant.

Broth with thoroughly browned little cubelets of bread is another pleasant introduction to the main course. Cut slices of bread in small cubes and brown them carefully in butter. Bring them to the table in a bowl and let each guest add them to his broth as he needs them. They should be thrown in a few at a time so that they will be partially crisp when lifted to the mouth. Cheese is necessary here, and a little minced parsley, chervil, or cress will add to the color and flavor.

Tiny meat balls will add character to the clear broth. They can be made easily and quickly. Mince whatever herbs you prefer, add them to ground round steak, bind with one egg and a bit of cheese. Brown the meat balls, about the size of a small cherry, in butter or olive oil. Drop them into the boiling broth and cook slowly for a few minutes. Serve five or six to each person. When more are requested, you display the empty pot and pass on to the next course.

When you make broth, the recipe given above may be doubled so that you may have plenty left over for use during the next week or ten days. Fine meat stock is indispensable in cookery, and the bouillon cube should be used as a substitute only in emergencies. If you make the broth today and serve a cupful preceding the dinner of boiled meat, tomorrow you may use a part of what is left for an excellent and nourishing dish: *Risotto,* of which there are two authentic ver﹐ sions, the Milanese and the Tuscan. Good broth is necessary for both.

For the Milanese, proceed as follows: Place in a skillet enough butter and olive oil in equal parts to cover the bottom. Add a large onion finely minced and cook slowly just short of browning. While the onion is cooking, add a handful of mushrooms cut in small pieces. If the dry ones are used they should be soaked for a few minutes in a cup of hot stock. (The mushroom-flavored stock will be later added to the rice.) Two quarts of stock should be heating while these ingredients are being prepared. When the onion and mushrooms have cooked sufficiently, throw in two cups (for six servings) of raw long-grain rice, washed and well drained. Stir briskly for two or three minutes over a medium fire. Avoid burning the rice, for if you do, it will become hard as granite and as difficult to cook. When the rice is well assimilated with the ingredients in the skillet, add enough of the hot broth barely to cover the rice. Give it a good stir, increase the heat and cover. As it begins to bubble and spurt, stir again so that the rice will not cling to the bottom. When the broth has been completely absorbed, add more, and repeat the above routine until the rice is cooked. Stir frequently, salt and pepper to taste, and don't leave the kitchen or you run the risk of complete failure.

When the rice is done it should be somewhat fluid, about the consistency of thinnish mush, so that when put on the dish it will slowly spread out. Before serving, stir in a piece of butter about the size of a lemon. Garnish as you please and pass the grated cheese that each guest may help himself. The Milanese dissolve a pinch of saffron in broth and add it to the rice before serving. I advise against it, and if you want to know the reason, try it once.

For the Tuscan version, these are the directions: Cut in very small pieces, about the size of a bean, half a pound of round steak, three or four chicken livers, and fry in oil and butter. Mince two or three sprigs of parsley, one of thyme, a few leaves of basil when in season, a very small onion, and a clove of garlic.

They must be minced to a pulp. Add to the meat and continue cooking over a slow fire for a few minutes. *The herbs should not be browned.* Add as many mushrooms as you please without, of course, losing your fine sense of proportion. Increase the fire and add a small tin of tomato sauce with double that amount of broth. Bring to a boil, then simmer for a few minutes. Put in the rice and proceed as for the Milanese recipe. When the rice is three-fourths done, add half a pound of raw spinach coarsely cut. Stir well and complete the cooking. The spinach may be omitted. Try it both ways. This dish, with salad, cheese, and your favorite dessert, is one of the most elegant among inexpensive dinners.

A final warning: *Risotto* is a dish that *must* be served immediately after it is cooked. If it stands for even a few minutes, the binding starches go to work and you have a mess on your hands. From first to last, it requires constant attention while cooking, with frequent stirring to keep it loose and fluid. Additional broth should be added the minute the preceding bath has been absorbed. And when you serve it, be certain it isn't too thick.

III

While at work in the fields during the summer months, the peasant in my native village always ate four meals a day: a light breakfast at sunrise, preceded by a snort of *acqua vite* if he could afford it, a heavy dinner at noon, a *merenda* late in the afternoon, and a light supper at dusk. The *merenda* was usually a heavy, nourishing peasant soup brought to the fields by one of the women. It was made with a variety of vegetables, frequently cooked in a bean broth, and eaten cold with onions and bread in the summer sun. Occasionally it was ladled over pieces of *polenta*. If it contained paste as an ingredient no bread was eaten with it. (Incidentally, eating bread with spaghetti or with soups containing paste is like eating mashed potatoes with French fries. It is a refinement unknown to the Italian peasant.)

Such soups, and others of the same general type, are traditional peasant fare throughout Europe. They are complete dinners, nourishing and full of flavor when made by expert hands not handicapped by lack of ingredients. They are the peasant's contribution to good living, and their humble origin should not cause the gourmet to turn up his nose at them. Eaten two or three times a month for the evening meal, perhaps more frequently when the necessary vegetables are in season, they will give pleasant relief from a diet of flesh, fish, and fowl. The sharp contrast will also add to the enjoyment of the next day's rib roast or top sirloin, while the genuine economy of such a dish will help to keep the budget balanced.

The *minestrone* is without doubt the most imposing as well as the most satisfying among all such peasant soups. Its very name has a pontifical ring which suggests the crowning dome of accomplishment. The men of Piedmont and Genoa, the fellow citizens of Columbus, Cavour, and Manzoni, the ancestors of the lantern-jawed colossus of the prize ring, were the inventors of this culinary extravaganza; and to this day, no one can match their skill in preparing it and their capacity in stowing it away. I have been making it and eating it for years with undiminished zest, but the best I have ever had was made by the wife of a Genoese truck farmer in suburban Portland, Oregon. It was in mid-August, and all the necessary ingredients were in luxuriant abundance in the immaculate garden adjoining the house. My hostess fed four men and three husky children, all of whom worked long hours in the sun; so the kettle she used was more like a washing machine than a kitchen utensil.

The base for *minestrone* is a bean broth. The appropriate beans are *fagioli romani*—Roman beans. In grocery stores where they are available, they are sometimes labeled cranberry or Oregon horticultural beans. In Italian groceries, where one will probably have to go to find them, they are known simply as Roman beans. Any bean, of course, will do, but the *romani* are the beans to use for genuine *minestrone*. The best time to go in for *minestrone* with a vengeance is in the early fall; for then one may not only procure all the necessary vegetables and herbs, but also fresh, ripe *romani* in the shell. In that state, their flavor is something to be long remembered. An enthusiastic guest once compared it to that of wild duck. If you properly discount the enthusiasm, the suggestion is not devoid of merit. Sprinkle them with salt and eat them as you would peanuts. Then make your own comparisons.

In a sense, *minestrone* is a seasonal as well as a regional dish. By using the dry beans and whatever vegetables are available, one may prepare it any time during the year; but if one wants the best it must be made in the early fall months, especially since fresh basil is the real secret of this extraordinary soup. I have never found a restaurant version which has not been a disgraceful phony. This is the recipe the truck gardener's wife gave to me, scaled down to human dimensions:

Bring out the master kettle and put in it six quarts of water, a small ham hock, and a quart of *romani* which have soaked over night. If you are using the fresh beans double the quantity and add them to the kettle when the ham has boiled for an hour. If *romani* are not available, the best substitutes are limas or kidney beans. When the beans are thoroughly cooked, lift them from the water, mash them through a strainer, and return them to the kettle. Remove the ham hock and use as you please.

Add to the broth the following combination of vegetables or as many of them as you can procure. I list them in the order of preference: Savoy cabbage, chard, tip ends of the pumpkin or zucchini vine, zucchini, celery, and a very few young chicory leaves. The tip ends of the zucchini vine will have small leaves about two inches in diameter, tiny zucchini with the open yellow blossoms, and green, closed flower buds. These tips in the soup will be worth the trouble entailed in procuring them. (No trouble at all if you have taken chapter four seriously.) The vegetables should be cut rather coarsely.

All vegetable soups, whether with or without a bean base, require a characteristic condiment. The ham hock is not enough. Something is required both to enhance and offset the flavor of the vegetable synthesis. Without the condiment, the soup is watery and bland. So while the beans are cooking, prepare the following sauce. Mince a quarter of a pound of lean salt pork. It must be so minced that it will spread as butter on bread. During the mincing, heat the edge of the cleaver occasionally so that the meat will not stick to it. As the meat spreads out on the board, keep turning and folding it toward the center. When the desired consistency is achieved, place it in a saucepan over a slow fire and fry it slowly without browning it too much. Then add to it three cloves of garlic and a large onion chopped fine. Continue cooking until browned very slightly. Add a large can of tomatoes or an equal quantity of fresh ones. Season with a bit of allspice and pepper and let it simmer for about three quarters of an hour. Then add this to the soup soon after the vegetables, which should cook no more than fifteen or twenty minutes. Recipes which specify that these soups should cook for several hours after the vegetables have been added are simply perpetuating a culinary error. The vegetables should be rather under than overdone. At this point, salt to taste.

I have left purposely vague the amount of vegetables to be used. There are some who insist that *minestrone* should be so thick that a spoon may stand upright in a bowl of it. Others prefer it in a more fluid state. So take your choice and use vegetables accordingly, remembering that paste—elbows, for example— three-fourths precooked must be added when the vegetables are nearly done. The amount of paste used (and remember that it increases in bulk like rice) will depend on whether you have decided on stew, or soup that may be partially inhaled.

The final benediction for *minestrone* is half a cup of fresh basil minced very fine and added two or three minutes before the soup is ladled into bowls. If you intend to use bread rubbed with garlic, don't use paste. When the guests have been served, pass around a bowl full of grated *Parmigiano.* No salad with this dinner. A dessert of fruit in season with your favorite cheese, coffee and brandy, will show your guests that you know your culinary way around.

For a more simple and very delightful soup, one that can be prepared in less than an hour, try the following variation on the *minestrone* theme: Make the sauce suggested for the above recipe directly in the soup kettle. Add to the sauce a spoonful of minced thyme. Cut the vegetables directly into the sauce and add as much boiling water as you need to attain the desired consistency. Salt to taste and add (or omit) paste as above. Serve with or without cheese. This *is* a lighter soup than *minestrone*, so a heavier dessert, such as pie, would be appropriate.

And here is another variation on the basic theme: Add to the above sauce some minced parsley and celery after the tomatoes. Cut only savoy cabbage into the sauce, add the necessary boiling water, and then stir in a tin of black bean soup. In three-quarters of an hour you will give your family a soup for which they will frequently ask. Serve it with buttered toast rubbed with lots of garlic.

For all these soups, the savoy cabbage, especially its outer green leaves, which have a slight bitter tang that blends perfectly with the bean broth, is much superior to the sweetish white cabbage. If savoy is not available, chard and a few turnip tops are an excellent substitute.

I have omitted from these soups such well-known vegetables as carrots, fresh peas, and string beans. Recipes for vegetable soups tend to be a bit reckless. They seem to be conceived on the erroneous assumption that the best vegetable soup is made by throwing the whole garden into the pot. Where there are beans in the soup, especially the shelled ones, string beans are a needless repetition. Peas and carrots are rather sweet and so destroy the characteristic flavor of the leaf vegetables recommended above. If one wants peas and carrots in a soup, let them predominate. Touch them up with a bit of spinach and celery. The soup will be good, but it will be different from the ones I have described above.

For the same reason beware, too, of those soup recipes which read something like this: "Throw into a huge kettle the turkey carcass and the ham bone. Add all oddments of vegetables found in the cooler and let them simmer gaily together while you play eighteen holes of golf. When you return from the fairways and eat your steak, throw the bones and whatever else is not consumed into the kettle. Eat it the next day and don't crack a smile." It is amazing the number of cookery books that go in for this blasé nonsense. *Pot au phooey,* indeed! I am waiting for someone with enough imagination to complete the recipe with the appropriate last line.

Pasta e fagioli—paste with beans—might well be substituted, on occasion, for a dinner of baked beans. It is a favorite soup among southern Italians whose passion for legumes is matched only by their enthusiasm for *maccheroni.* This is the way I like it best: Soak a pound of navy beans for twelve hours and then cook them slowly in three quarts of water. During the last half-hour add two or three sprigs of thyme. When the beans are nearly cooked, flavor with the following condiment: mince two cloves of garlic and a little parsley in three tablespoonfuls of olive oil and cook for about one minute very slowly. Add a small tin of tomato sauce and an equal amount of water. Simmer for twenty minutes and add to the beans. Partially precook some paste, such as elbows, *ditalini,* or small sea shells, in lots of water. Drain and add to the beans when they are completely cooked. Let the two simmer together for about ten minutes, salt and pepper to taste, and serve with grated cheese. Don't mess up this dinner with salads or other vegetables. This is strictly in defiance of the dietitian. If you don't think it is sufficiently balanced, gorge yourself on spinach the following day.

Garlic bread is steadily making new friends. If you like it, try it with this strictly seasonal soup: Mince a bit of ham—say half a pound—in enough butter and olive oil to cover the bottom of a skillet. Add a clove of garlic, an onion, and some parsley minced. Cook slowly for two or three minutes, then add three large, ripe tomatoes. Let the whole simmer about twenty minutes. Put in a quart of fresh, shelled *romani* and about half a quart of string beans. Add enough boiling water to attain a soupy consistency. Cook slowly until done. During the last ten minutes add a dozen or so leaves of fresh basil. The soup should be thick though rather fluid, so regulate the water accordingly. This dish is thoroughly satisfying, and I know none other for which buttered toast rubbed with garlic is so indispensable an accompaniment.

My final suggestion is a tripe soup highly esteemed by the inhabitants of the Po valley. The principal ingredients are tripe and lima beans. For six people use three pounds of tripe and a pound of beans. Proceed in this manner: Remove globules of fat from the tripe, wash it thoroughly and boil it for half an hour in enough water to cover. Drain and dry it well with a cloth. Mince to a pulp one-fifth of a pound of lean salt pork or ham. Fry it slowly in the kettle in which the soup is to be made. Drain off some of the fat and add two tablespoonfuls of butter. Mince an onion, a bit of parsley, a stalk of celery, and two cloves of garlic. Cook them briefly with the pork over a slow fire, then add a small tin of tomato sauce. Simmer for ten minutes, then add the tripe cut in very thin strips. Put in enough boiling water to produce a soupy consistency and cook slowly for about two hours. At that time add the lima beans, which have been cooked separately until nearly done, salt and pepper to taste, and let the whole simmer together for another half-hour. The beans should be cooked in just enough water to keep them moist, so that when they are added to the tripe, the bean broth will be rather thick. Serve with croutons and grated *Parmigiano*.

3

Please, My Name Is Angelo

AT THE age of eleven, somewhat rugged and hefty for my years, curiously and cleanly appareled, a heavy watch chain snaked across my little round belly, I entered the first grade in an American country school.

The first decade of my life had been crowded with a variety of experience. I had already worked for wages and as an independent enterpriser. I had known the sting of the peasant's whip and the horror of being chased by men who guarded their orchards with pruning hook and scythe. I had seen a maniac slit the throat of the village cobbler as he sat at his last in the August sun eating watermelon. A neighbor had dropped dead at my feet as we worked together breaking clods of earth in the plowed field.

I had seen men and women in strange postures between rows of tall tasseled corn, and had had no difficulty in equating the spectacle to what I had observed among animals engaged in "the deed of kind."

I had known the meaning, if not the words that express it, of the struggle for survival. When Father had gone abroad in search of work and had failed to write for several months, I had seen Mother, normally lithe and strong and happy, reduced to skin and bones with worry. In her tears, which she sought vainly to conceal from us children, I had seen, too early in life, the terrible meaning of black despair.

I had crossed the Atlantic in an uncertain bottom that on several occasions seemed a likely victim to the heavy anarchy of wind and waves. I had known the inexcusable cruelty of Ellis Island. Tagged and labeled like a piece of baggage, I had traveled across the North American continent at the complete mercy of public servants who seemed wholly indifferent to my eager, tortured, bewildered existence. At the end of the journey had been reunion with Father, a comfortable home, and the fulfillment of a dream.

Thus experienced beyond my years, I should have entered the first grade with Dante's bitter, cynical smile, balanced by the gaiety and confidence implicit in the future that lay before me. It was all otherwise! Although I could have eaten any three of my classmates for breakfast, I was self-conscious, confused, disappointed, and terribly frightened. Where I had anticipated the kindness and courtesy a stranger may fairly expect from his Christian fellows, I received the taunts and jeers and verbal insults of tough little sons and hard little daughters of frontier loggers. I was the first child they had ever met who could not speak their language, and they fell to the opportunity like vultures to carnage.

There was one among them who was a living refutation of such sentimental slop as "No man is wholly bad." An autopsy, I am sure, would have revealed him rotten to the core. He was an older boy, strong, square-headed, and brutal, who found the second grade so fascinating that he was repeating it for the fourth year. I do not remember a single instance when that unfortunate perversion of *homo sapiens* was engaged in some act of kindness and generosity. "No man is wholly bad." Bah!

This ambassador of good will received me daily or the school grounds and escorted me home in the afternoon. His favorite trick was to set verbal traps into which, of course, I easily fell. He would gather his satellites about him, corner me in some convenient spot, and then proceed with the following routine: "Is your mother a whore? Are you a sonofabitch, dago, wop, garlic, spaghetti?"

Since I understood only the last word and conjectured that the rest must have been an elaborate invitation to dinner, my usual reply was an enthusiastic pantomimic affirmative. When I had thus assured him of my total depravity, he would assume his instinctive posture and start throwing left and right jabs in my general direction. The whole performance was so confusing, so unintelligible, that I could only smile sickly and retreat from his blows.

But there came a reckoning. On the way home from school we had to cross a railroad track, and on a memorable day a gang of Italians were working at the crossing. Among them was one who had a fair knowledge of the English language. Eager to amuse a new audience, the towheaded bully made his fatal mistake: he repeated and enlarged upon his performance in the presence of those men who were my father's friends.

That evening they gathered at my home and I was given a complete translation of the abuse that had been heaped upon me. "*Brutte bestie,*" I muttered over and over. What was I to do? There was really no choice. I was told that in America one fights for his rights; that the alternative is constant abuse and unsparing ridicule; that once you have beaten a man to a pulp, he becomes your best friend. (This last still seems altogether preposterous.)

The young man who knew America best cautioned me against the use of weapons he knew I was contemplating in silence. "Here," he said, "we fight with the fist. We blacken the eyes, smash the nose, knock out the teeth. If the adversary falls, we stand back, give him a chance to get to his feet, then smack him down again. When he says he's licked, we shake hands, drink together, and forget the whole damned thing."

Before I could blurt out the equivalent of "Who, me?" the most forthright and least speculative among those good men suggested that on the morrow I had better take a pick handle to school with me. I must confess that the advice seemed to me exceedingly prudent.

Well, we had finally decided upon "the purple testament of bleeding war" as the only honorable retaliation to the insults I had endured, when my father, who instinctively recoiled from all unpleasantness, suggested that we throw out "peace feelers." He argued, plausibly, that the boy was probably irritated because I had never really answered his question. He wanted to know my name. Why not tell him courteously and await results? That seemed fair enough.

So, anticipating a well-known prime minister, we shifted to a policy of "peace for our time." Accordingly, we agreed that when the bully should again ask his filthy questions, I should simply answer "Please, my name is Angelo," and conclude with, what under the circumstances was forgivable tautology, "My mother is a good lady." I memorized the two short sentences and went to bed.

To sleep? No, to sob my way out of confusion. Why should anyone, entirely unprovoked, take advantage of my ignorance of the language to make such an utter fool of me? Couldn't they see that I wanted friends, desired to learn? And my mother a whore? She whose patient endurance of sadness and adversity had been so heroic? And why did they call me *spaghetti? **Po-***

lenta or *minestrone* would have been more understandable. Thinking on pruning hooks and pick handles, I finally fell asleep.

The following day I clenched my fists and went off to school. On the way home, as predictable as he was stupid and mean, the little giant of the second grade went through his nauseous song and dance. Humbly and with faultless articulation, I repeated the two short sentences I had so diligently learned. His reaction was precisely what I had expected and for which I was thoroughly prepared.

"Oh, no! You are sonofabitch, dago—"

Before he could rape Czechoslovakia I had lunged at his throat and sent him sprawling to the ground. With incredible swiftness I gave him a hammer blow on the nose and banged his head several times on the hard, stony ground. He was bleeding profusely and a little stunned. I suppose I should have helped him to his feet and knocked him down again. I had been told that was the accepted procedure, a fact for which I was later to discover an abundance of cinematographic confirmation. But the process of Americanization isn't instantaneous. I simply left him there and fled home, trembling with fear.

That was the beginning and not the end of my troubles. For the next four years, with wit and fist, I fought a slowly advancing engagement toward the objective I never lost sight of for a single moment— to be accepted as "one of the boys." With dramatic propriety, two events brought the final victory. Within the compass of a single day I placed second in a spelling contest and pitched the school team to victory over the "whistle punks" from the near-by logging village.

The word that had stumped me in the spelling contest was "sizzers." That is the way I spelled it and I am yet to be convinced that I was wrong. But no matter. Second place was good enough for me. Soon thereafter, those who had once ridiculed me made me president of the Epworth League and captain of the ball team. That *was* the end of my troubles. I had become an American—"one of the boys."

II

No one had been able to explain to my satisfaction why the permanent second-grader had included *spaghetti* in the series of abusive names with which he had sought to identify me. I knew the word neither as a term of derision nor as the name of a dish. And that is not surprising, for it is the inventive, ineffable American—the most adept of all mortals at phrase-making and verbal short cuts—that has given the word both those meanings.

In America, spaghetti is now a well-established, quasi-national dish. The "spaghetti dinner" is American terminology and American practice. In Italian cuisine there is no such thing as a "spaghetti dinner." And as for tinned spaghetti, without any doubt at the apex of culinary atrocities, it is as American as the hot dog.

Predictions, in this most uncertain of all possible worlds, are the amusement of fools. Let me join their ranks and hazard this: America's gastronomic coming of age will be heralded by a national uprising against tinned spaghetti. Unfortunately, at the moment, the horizon reflects a profound satisfaction with the *status quo*.

Let us attempt to set the record straight. In Italian cuisine, *pasta* is a basic staple. It is the generic name for all macaroni products that may be seen in various patterns or cuts in Italian groceries. Names such as

164

lasagne, vermicelli, cappellini, etc., are descriptive of the patterns into which the *pasta* is cut. Thus, the name *spaghetti,* a derivative of *spago,* the Italian word for heavy twine, refers not to a dish, but to one of the numerous *pasta* patterns.

When *pasta,* whether homemade or fabricated, is boiled, drained, and served with any one of an endless variety of sauces or condiments and grated cheese, it is called *pasta al sugo* or more commonly, *pasta asciutta*—literally, dry paste. This distinguishes it from *pasta al brodo* or *minestrone*—paste in broth or various soup combinations.

The heaviest patterns, such as *cannelloni,* tubular pieces about three-quarters of an inch in diameter and two inches long, are more frequently served *al sugo;* the finer, such as *cappellini,* are served in broth. Spaghetti is as often cooked in soups as *al sugo.* Everyone has his preference in patterns, but the principle of selection is universally recognized: use for *pasta asciutta* the patterns that absorb the greatest quantity of sauce.

The quality of the *pasta* is of first importance. The best is made with durum wheat *semolina.* It is best because when cooked for approximately twenty minutes it is firm, free from sticky starches, and retains its shape. *Pasta* made with ordinary wheat flour is a phony, and no Italian will use it. It "mushes" up, falls apart, and sticks to the teeth. There is plenty of durum wheat in America, and many experienced Italian macaroni manufacturers to put it to good use. Since there are also the usual impostors—*caveat emptor!*

The cooking of the *pasta* is also important. It should be dropped in an abundance of boiling, salted water —enough so that the *pasta* may freely squirm and writhe in it—and cooked *al dente;* that is, until it is no longer granular, but soft enough to be chewed with ease and yet firm enough to offer some resistance to the teeth. This should take about twenty minutes. To avoid overcooking, however, it is advisable to taste it frequently. When it is done, more very hot water is added, the *pasta* is swirled around with a fork a few times to wash off the excess starch, and drained immediately by tossing and whirling in a spacious colander. It is then ready for the sauce and the cheese.

What cheese? The answer is one of the few culinary absolutes: *Romano* and *Parmigiano*. The first is sharp; the second mild. My preference is an even blend of the two. The grated imitations sold in attractive little packets should be studiously avoided. It is best to buy a chunk of the cheese and grate it when needed.

What sauce? There are so many sauces and condiments for *pasta* that one may have it every day in the year without a single duplication. They may be divided for convenience into two main categories: *al grasso* and *al magro*—meat and meatless sauces. The division is a perfectly natural one in Italy, where both scarcity and religion affect the diet so intimately.

Sauces *al grasso* vary according to the meat and herbs used in the preparation. What I shall call the basic sauce is made with round steak and mushrooms. Since *pasta asciutta* is most frequently served as a part of the Sunday and holiday dinner, when fowl or rabbit is usually the meat course, the giblets of the fowl or the heart, liver, and kidneys of the rabbit are normally added to the sauce. They considerably enhance both its consistency and flavor.

The procedure is by no means definitive. If I leave something out of the recipe, it is because I have given one rather than another variation on an exceedingly elastic theme. For six portions of pasta, one pound of round steak is cut into thin, longitudinal strips and then cut again into little pieces about the size of a pea. If the giblets of the fowl or heart, kidneys, and liver of the rabbit are used, these are cut and added to the meat, which is then browned quickly in enough butter or olive oil to cover the bottom of the sauce pan. Next, two cloves of garlic and a medium onion are minced and cooked for a few minutes with the meat, taking care not to brown them. To these are added a cup of fresh or a handful of dry mushrooms. If the latter are used, they are first soaked for five minutes in a cup of boiling water, which is saved and added to the sauce later.

Next are added a large can of tomatoes—or its equivalent, if the fresh, ripe ones are used—and a small tin of some good tomato sauce, diluted in one cup of stock. The water in which the mushrooms were soaked, when the dry ones are used, enriched with a bouillon cube, may be substituted for the stock. The heat is then increased, salt, pepper, a touch of cayenne, a dash or two of allspice are added, and the pan is covered until the sauce begins to boil. The heat is then decreased, the cover removed from the pan, and the sauce is left to simmer for about two hours. It is stirred now and then to prevent sticking and to aid the evaporation.

Fifteen or twenty minutes before the sauce is done, a few sprigs of parsley, three or four leaves of fresh sage, a teaspoonful of thyme, and the rind of a quarter of a lemon are minced very fine and added. The final benediction, immediately after the herbs, is three-quarters of a cup of dry sherry or, if sherry is not on hand, some good white wine.

The simmering of the sauce is important. Its function is to metamorphose the tomato, secure the maximum assimilation of the ingredients, and achieve considerable dehydration. When the tomato and liquids are added, the sauce is very fluid and quite red; when done, it should be rather thick and dark.

The *pasta*—a pound and a half for six portions—properly cooked and thoroughly drained, is placed in the large kettle in which it was boiled and half the sauce is thrown over it. With two large forks it is tossed briskly until the sauce is evenly distributed. During the tossing, which should be done with the kettle over a slow fire, three or four spoonfuls of cheese are added. The *pasta* is then spread upon a warm serving platter and the remainder of the sauce is spooned evenly over it. With a final sprinkling of cheese over the whole—*Ecco, la pasta asciutta!*

This basic recipe, simple and inexpensive, yields a superb sauce. When prepared in this way it cannot be hurried. Two hours are the absolute minimum. The assembling of the ingredients, if one knows his way around the kitchen, should not take more than thirty minutes. The stove does the rest of the work.

The possible variations immediately suggest themselves. There are other herbs: rosemary, marjoram, basil. There are capers. There are other spices. There are other meats that may be used singly or in combinations. Sauce for *pasta* is ever in a state of becoming. Mothers who have been making it one way and another for half a century are still asking each other, of a Sunday evening: "*E oggi come l'avete fatta la salza?*"—And how did you make your sauce today? The world is still waiting to acclaim the creator of the definitive sauce. So get busy.

And if you are interested in achievement with a capital A, you might investigate with profit the sauces latent in rabbit, game birds, and fowl. For this venture you could do worse than choose the Florentines or Lucchesi as your guides. When they bag their limit of quail, snipe, pheasant, or whatnot, they think instinctively of the excellent sauce they will have for the *pasta asciutta*.

I no longer hunt, because hunting has become a luxury and a hazard. Men once hunted because they needed meat; now most men hunt for the exercise and the "sport," not to mention other reasons more intimate and personal. The hunting season calls to the hills and the prairies men who have no need for the game they seek, and who now and then mistake each other for the horned animal upon whom they collectively prey. Under the circumstances, I am not in the least tempted to travel several hundred miles and to fight my way over forbidding terrain for the dubious pleasure of being mistaken for an elk. So I stay at home.

And have my share of game, too. Mallards are occasionally sent to me from a thousand miles away. Many hunters, and the families of many hunters, have no relish for the game that is so laboriously bagged. Let them try a sauce for *pasta* made in some such way as this: Cut two mallards—or any other specie of wild duck—into very small pieces and brown them in enough olive oil and butter to cover the bottom of a skillet of adequate size. Remove the meat to a bowl and set it aside. Now, using half the amount of round steak, make the sauce in the skillet according to the recipe given above. When the tomato is added, return the pieces of duck to the sauce and simmer slowly for about three hours. When the sauce is done, the pieces of game are removed, kept warm, and served with the desired cooked vegetable after the *pasta*. The friends who keep me supplied with game, if they could ever be persuaded to try this recipe . . . But what am I saying? Come next autumn, I want my mallards.

All game, including venison and elk, may be used

for this purpose and in much the same manner. According to a good friend who fed me so elegantly when first we met that I shall never forget the occasion, wild duck, rabbit, elk, and deer should marinate over night in a mild tarragon vinegar before they are used for sauce or cooked in any other way. He ought to know; for he is a Lucchese, a hunter, a fisherman, and a gourmet of unusual gusto and good sense.

A thinner, less substantial, but very savory sauce may be made by using the drippings from a roast—any roast—after the fat has been removed. This is a sauce *alla scappata*—made very quickly, while the roast is being kept warm in the oven. To the drippings one adds tomato sauce—not tomatoes—diluted with stock, minced herbs, garlic, and mushrooms. A brisk simmering for twenty minutes or so and it is done. The *pasta* may then be served as a substitute for potatoes, with the roast.

All meat sauces may be given a distinctive flavor by the use, in small quantities, of *conserva di pomidoro,* a hard, dryish tomato paste that, unfortunately, is rarely available even in the most exclusive food shops. The commercial tomato paste is an altogether inadequate substitute. Those of us who find it difficult to do without *conserva* make our own. The process requires several days.

In mid-August, when the sun is very hot, if you enjoy bringing good things into being, cook thirty pounds of ripe tomatoes in the master kettle, and add thereto a bunch of fresh parsley and an equal amount of fresh basil. Use an abundance of salt, since it aids in the preservation of the paste. When cooked for about two hours, drain in a colander to get rid of the water. Then force the residue through a strainer with holes about an eighth of an inch in diameter. Keep rubbing it through with the hands until only the skins and seeds remain. Spread the paste on a large platter and set it out in the sun to dehydrate. When it can be shaped into a ball it is sufficiently dry. If the sun is very hot, this should not take more than three days. The paste, packed in half-pint jars and sealed with a layer of olive oil, may be kept several years. I am currently using *conserva* made two years ago.

It is used rather sparingly in cooking. A teaspoonful dissolved in stock would be ample as a supplement for the tomatoes and a substitute for the tomato sauce prescribed for the basic recipe. Half that amount is enough to lend distinction to any sauce for fish or meat when tomato is an ingredient.

I have suggested a pound and a half of *pasta* for six servings. The amount is rather arbitrary. Any given six persons may eat more or less than that before they settle down to the meat course. Some people have an inordinate capacity for certain foods. Among Italians, there are men and women, otherwise normal, who are reputed eaters of *pasta asciutta*. My own father, the most temperate of men at the table, once ate two pounds after dinner on a wager. He won a barrel of Chianti and lived merrily to enjoy it. Merely to think upon the deed makes me pop my buttons!

The best advice, accordingly, can be no more explicit than this: Know your capacity and proceed with discretion. One ought to bear in mind that *pasta* increases in bulk as it cooks and that it satiates the average person rather quickly. When one looks at a pound and a half uncooked, it may seem a trifle; when it is ready for the table, it is not likely that any four individuals chosen at random could eat the whole of it comfortably. Let us merely say, then, by way of conclusion, that the sauce which the basic recipe will yield is not adequate for more than a pound and a half of *pasta*. If the table is to be surrounded by Falstaffian girths, the sauce recipe should be doubled.

III

Those who have followed me to this page and understood what I have been trying to say, will certainly know that I prefer good bread and cheese to an elaborate dinner prepared with a perverse imagination. What I most abhor about travel in rural America is the desecrated food that one must endure —not infrequently dispensed by foreigners who should know better. Good meat, potatoes, and vegetables blighted by some rude hand behind the counter or in the unseen kitchen are to me positively revolting.

Fortunately, in such matters I am not easily defeated. When, as it happened recently, I must leave the hearth for an extended period, I fall back upon an innate resourcefulness and so find salvation. I keep myself supplied with bread, cheese, and raw vegetables. In restaurants I rarely abandon an old favorite—ham and eggs. (I have long since given up trying to tell a cook, through a waitress, how to prepare my eggs. They just don't understand.) Occasionally, by diligent search, I find an Italian family with whom I make myself at home. I have always lived in the presumptuous, though comforting notion that any Italian, anywhere, has been waiting to welcome me with open arms. I must say that I have been fortunate beyond my deserts.

At any rate, it was some such combination of impertinence and an implicit belief in the fellowship of man that brought me to the threshold of a well-known Italian in Kellogg, Idaho. When I arrived in that picturesque frontier mining town of the West to fulfill lecture engagements, I had been away from home for two months. I had lost some weight. I was ready to Eat. The usual inquiries led to this *paesano,* and I barged in.

Italians are notoriously adept at such subterfuge and indirection as "Is it possible to buy a good glass of wine and some real bread in this town?" meaning: I would be delighted to have dinner with you.

That is precisely the question I put to the stranger who became my friend. The reply, of course, was not unexpected. "There is no need to look further. The Signora bakes excellent bread. I have plenty of wine, such as it is. We have *prosciutto,* tuna in olive oil, and homemade sausage. We can fry a steak. A little salad—"

"Oh, no, no, no, *please,*" I lied, "I have just eaten." They knew the formula and would have been disappointed had I not repeated it.

"Well, then," said my host, "he who has eaten must drink. Let me pour you a glass of wine. It's an indifferent vintage. But you know how it is. Here among the mountains we have to be satisfied with what we can get. *Salute.*"

"*Salute. Per la Madonna,* this is an excellent wine," I said, when I had drained the glass with impressive dispatch. I could tell by the smile on his face as he watched me drink it, that he too knew it was an excellent wine. It's good manners, a part of the formula, to be modest about one's wine and to let the guest judge its merits.

"I can see that milk hasn't ruined your palate. You're quite right. The wine isn't bad. In fact, it's the best wine I have had since I left Lucca thirty-five years ago. I made it five years ago from grapes a friend sent me from Sonoma County in California. Doesn't it seem to you that it has some of the character of Chianti?"

As he reached to pour me another glass I became increasingly aware of genuine hunger. I continued with the formula which, I knew, had about served its purpose. "Please, just a drop. Ho, *per Bacco*, that's too much!"

"*Bevi, Pellegrini, senza far complimenti.*" He urged me to accept his hospitality without "making compliments," that is, without graciously expressed reluctance. But, of course, one is expected to be graciously reluctant—*far complimenti*—for that gives the host an opportunity to become eloquent about his hospitality; and eloquence is necessary to a Latin, indispensable to an Italian.

"I am glad you like that wine. I have a dozen bottles left. If you are free tomorrow I will take a day off. I have some fine rabbits. A friend, just a short distance away, always has fresh brook trout on hand. *Senza far complimenti . . .*"

The Signora, who had been in the kitchen, came into the living room bearing a tray laden with grilled sausage, thinly sliced *prosciutto*, tuna in olive oil, radishes, celery, olives, and a basket of the finest bread I have ever eaten. "He who drinks,'" said my host, "must eat."

The comedy of manners was over. It was midnight, and we settled down to the feast. Two days later, with a visibly increased girth, I left that rugged country to complete my circuit.

In another village—"On instinct," sir!—I found my way to the shop of an Italian cobbler. His appearance was immediately reassuring. An enormous body was topped by a full, round face, brightened by laughing eyes and what appeared to be a permanent smile. A cigar clenched firmly between the teeth and right under the nose, rounded out the portrait of a man who, I knew, lived well and liked it.

It was about dinnertime, so I identified myself and asked the usual question. "Where in this town may a man get a decent dinner?"

He spread a little more widely the smile that was a part of his face. "If you will excuse the humble surroundings and the general untidiness—you see, my wife has gone on a L-O-N-G vacation." The toss of the head, the inflection, and the twinkle in his eyes clearly indicated that he was a merry bachelor. He leaned forward, as if to say something in confidence, the cigar still clenched between the teeth. "I have a fine porterhouse in the cooler. There is an abundance of wine. Salad greens are in the garden. In half an hour I can prepare some *pasta*. If you will do me the honor, I will immediately close the shop. My poor feet have been carrying this carcass for ten hours. They need a rest. Come back into the kitchen and we'll have a vermouth."

While the *pasta* was boiling, he prepared a simple *al magro* sauce. A quarter of a pound of butter, a small tin of tomato sauce, three cloves of garlic finely minced, salt, pepper, a dash of allspice, and a cup of stock—that was all. It simmered for twenty or thirty minutes, by which time the *pasta* was cooked. With plenty of *Parmigiano*, it was very good. We ate a pound, then turned with whetted appetite to the porterhouse and salad.

As many of my American friends know from experience, immigrants as hospitable as my hosts are waiting to be discovered all over America. But, of course, one must know the formula.

Two of the most renowned versions of *al magro pasta asciutta* are the culinary contributions of the northern Italians: *pasta al burro* and *pasta al pesto*. Each requires a lot of butter, a fact that explains why

It is indigenous to the North, the center of the dairy industry.

The recipe for *pasta al burro* is exceedingly simple. While the *pasta* is draining, melt a third of a pound of butter (for six portions) in a large kettle. Keep it over a slow fire and toss the *pasta* in it briskly until the butter is evenly distributed. During the tossing, throw in three or four spoonfuls of cheese. Add, if you like, some minced parsley. Serve very hot with plenty of cheese over each serving.

For *pasta al pesto,* proceed as above, adding to the melted butter the following herb sauce: For a pound and a half of *pasta,* mince four cloves of garlic and enough fresh basil to fill a cup. The traditional method is to reduce them to a paste in mortar and pestle, with the addition of small quantities of olive oil as needed. I have never used these implements, but I have achieved, I am sure, the same results with a sharp, heavy, straight-edged knife. A bit of patience and a little time are required, for the mincing must be thorough.

Al pesto is a strictly seasonal dish. The basil *must* be fresh from the garden. According to my taste, it is also the best of all varieties of *pasta asciutta.* When I eat it I am never actually satiated. I simply stop eating when my jaws are fatigued and I can no longer masticate with ease. What further recommendation is needed for the dish?

In addition to these, there are various other *al magro* sauces. Any desirable combination of herbs, with olive oil and butter, with or without tomato, will yield highly palatable dressings for *pasta.* To list them would be tedious and, I think, a trifle unfair to cooks who like to be given credit for some imagination.

Italians along the coast, and especially Sicilians and Neapolitans, have developed a whole category of *al magro* sauces with sea food as a basic ingredient—crab, lobster, tuna (tinned), anchovies, clams, squid, and fresh water eel. The Tuscans make an exceptional sauce with frog meat.

These sauces all require olive oil and butter, as much garlic as one desires, and such herbs as tarragon, parsley, chervil and *puleggio*—pennyroyal. Tomato is optional in all of them and is used as a variant. They are prepared essentially like the basic sauce described earlier in this chapter. They all have merit.

I want to conclude the story of *pasta asciutta* with what I consider a culinary extravaganza—*la tortelleta*. It comes from the delightful kitchen of my young surgeon friend, Doctor Leo Rosellini. This singular young man, when not absorbed in researches for the cure of hyperthyroidism and related ailments, loves to eat and to entertain with abandon. When he wants an exceptional dinner, he calls his mother to his kitchen. Then he bustles in, in shirt sleeves and apron, and by appearing very busy and giving suggestions to which his mother indulgently listens and promptly disregards, he creates the happy illusion of being the culinary director.

This is the way to prepare *la tortelleta*—so far as I know, original in the Rosellini kitchen. Mince very fine the meat of one-third of a boiled chicken, including giblets. Put the meat in a spacious bowl. Add the rind of half a lemon and two cups of cooked, thoroughly drained spinach well minced. Add three raw eggs, half a cup of *Parmigiano*, and mix all the ingredients together. Add this to the basic sauce for *pasta asciutta* and let it simmer slowly for fifteen minutes. The recipe is adequate for a pound and a half of *pasta*. Use the sauce as a dressing for *lasagne*. The results, I assure you, will be amazing.

I must confess that I find *la tortelleta* in sauce for

pasta a little redundant. It is the natural reaction of a man whose taste in food is essentially simple, though —or so I like to believe—cultivated. There is, however, an alternative use for it—as an ingredient in chicken broth. You will discover, as I have, that a finer soup has yet to be created.

Among the Italians whom I know best, the Tuscans, it is heresy to drink wine with *pasta asciutta*. I have searched diligently and without success for the origin of this strange aberration in a people whose gastronomy is singularly devoid of superstition and myth. I can conjure no reason, either dietary or gastronomic, in defense of the practice. The Unprejudiced Palate has tried *pasta asciutta* both with clear, sparkling water and with clear, sparkling wine. My judgment is irrevocable. The reader will have no difficulty in guessing what it is.

4

Fish Must Be
Drowned in Wine

CHILDHOOD IN Italy in the early years of the present century was hard and exciting. Compared to that of the children of today, or even of a quarter century ago, it must seem to have been wholly devoid of fun. There were neither comics nor movies nor organized athletics. There were no weekly allowances, no mechanical toys, no excursions in motorcars to the mountains and seashore. There were no nursery rhymes to satisfy the child's eager imagination, no cupboards and coolers stocked with goodies to satisfy his lusty appetite.

It was a hard and barren childhood. And yet it was exciting, and fundamentally instructive. If we wanted a little wagon for amusement, with our own hands we hewed the wheels and axle out of precious wood that first had to be found somewhere. We made our own kites and devised our own games. We haunted birds' nests for meat to flavor the sauce for *pasta*, and we combed the countryside in search of food and fuel. When these expeditions yielded results, we experienced early in life the thrill of significant accomplishment. A penny earned in selling bundles of grass to draymen in the early morning, or a yard of sand to the mason, filled us with a sense of personal achievement. We were big little men proud of our contribution to the family's needs.

Even our occasional delinquencies were functional rather than moral aberrations. They were rooted in the needs of the stomach and not in the desire for new thrills to relieve a pampered existence. We raided the neighbor's fields for Windsor beans and fruit because we were forbidden to eat our own. The neighbor's children, who were just as hungry as we and who lived in the shadow of the same injunction, stole from us. We were cuffed and switched, often mercilessly, when caught in the act; while our parents inflicted the same punishment on the little urchins caught trespassing on our own property. It was a perfectly just arrangement, achieved without consultation and accepted all around in good grace. What our parents lost to the neighbor's brood we children recovered and gave to our ravenous stomachs. The border raids were exciting and dangerous.

There were two ventures in the struggle for existence which were particularly thrilling. The one was raiding birds' nests high up in the tallest trees; the other was catching fish with our bare hands. The birds, too, adjusted to the environment. To escape the predatory children, some of them nested on the highest branches of tall trees, bare of limbs three-quarters of the way up. When we were reasonably certain that a bird was nesting on a given tree, we made the exploratory climb, always perilous and arduous. Once the nest was spotted, the tree was climbed at intervals until we could predict when the nestlings would be about ready to fly. We seldom miscalculated. The final climb always yielded the precious reward brought joyfully home to an appreciative family.

To one who had regularly caught fish with his bare hands in an uneven struggle with the slippery creatures, the American fishhook seemed an unintelligible

piece of primitivism. As I fish the waters of Puget
Sound and the bays and inlets of the San Juan Islands
with plugs and spoons and pop gear, I am still a bit
incredulous about the efficacy of the means employed.
Even a forty-pound king salmon, safely landed in the
canoe, leaves me wondering about how he could have
been so foolish as to swallow a piece of wood with
six treacherous hooks dangling from its under side.

When I was a child, we caught fish in a rock-ribbed
river that was conveniently shallow during the summer months. The fish were frequently found in horizontal holes along the rocky banks of the stream.
Fresh-water eels, too, occasionally sought refuge in
such holes. All we had to do was wade the stream,
thrust our arms deep into the watery crevices, and
bring out the prize. Too often, what felt and acted
like an eel turned out to be a black, slithery water
snake. When that happened, the impostor was killed
with dispatch and the lad returned grimly to his business. For eels, however, we had homemade traps
which we set in the river bed. They were equipped
with funnel-shaped inlets and, to the eel, no perceptible way of escape.

Another means of catching fish was to chase them
in shallow pools where they could be readily caught
with the bare hands. One of the lads, armed with a
long bamboo pole that had a circular piece of leather
about four inches in diameter nailed to one end, would
start at a point downstream about five hundred yards
from the shallow pool and walk gradually toward it,
plunging his pole into the water as he went along.
That drove the fish into the trap, where another lad,
skilled in the business, caught them with his hands.
We were frequently frustrated, especially when the
depth of the water made such means doubly difficult;

so you may well imagine the pride with which we marched into the house and presented the fish to Mother when our efforts had been successful.

There were other sources of simple joy which we looked forward to from year to year. One was the yearly trip to market in mid-June to dispose of silkworm cocoons. The traditional reward for having assisted in feeding the silkworms was a basket of the first ripe cherries, a treat beyond the appreciation of this generation's pampered children.

Another was the cornhusking in the fall, always a community enterprise, followed by a dance in the clay courtyard. A veritable mountain of ears of corn, with the entire community seated in a circle at its base, everyone a skilled husker, would miraculously disappear in but a few hours. The work was so perfectly distributed and efficiently done that when the last ear was husked, the corn was in the bins, the fodder in the barn, and the courtyard cleared and swept for the dance.

The excitement for us children consisted in being permitted to stay up late, in bringing the tough ears of corn from the weaklings who couldn't husk them to the village strong man who did nothing but supplement the labors of his inadequate fellows, and in observing the strange behavior of our elders during the dance. We were to learn later that the name for it was "love."

Then there was *la svinatura*—the drawing of the wine from the fermenting vats and the pressing of the mash. That, too, was a task at which the neighbors assisted, and always an occasion for fun and frolic, especially when the vintage was up to expectations. There was simple food, presently to be described; but the emphasis was on song and drink, since the one cost nothing and the other was in abundance. The new wine had to be repeatedly tasted and compared with the yield of previous years before final judgment could be passed. Since the new product was slightly sweet and fruity, and therefore satisfied the peasant's hunger for sugar, the tasting far exceeded the limits of necessity.

The favorite song form for such an occasion was the *stornello*, extemporized couplets or quatrains sung to traditional folk tunes. The singing was done mostly by *stornellatrici*, men and women who operated in pairs and who were talented in quick and witty repartee as well as in song. One would lead off by stating a theme in a couplet sung to an agreed tune; whereupon the other would take up the challenge and answer with an appropriate couplet. Each played his own accompaniment on his guitar. There was, of course, much double talk, to which the language lends itself so marvelously, innuendo and allusion to topical material that baffled the children and made the elders laugh with reckless abandon.

For an occasion such as *la svinatura*, the launching couplet might well have been something like this:

> *Se voi venir, Morina, a stornellare,*
> *Porta del vino e mettiti a sedere*

If you would engage in singing *stornelli*, Morina, bring forth the wine and make yourself comfortable. Whereupon the other would answer:

> *Se io ti do da bere e da mangiare*
> *Tu con stornelli farmi incitrullire.*

If I provide you with food and drink, you must dazzle and amaze me with your *stornelli*. And so this lyrical feud would go on and on until both the theme and the *stornellatrici* were completely exhausted.

The food served at *la svinatura* was simple and salty designed to make the guests return frequently to the wine jug. There were dry, salted olives, *pizza* loaded with anchovies, and always quantities of dry, salted cod prepared and served thus: It was soaked in water for about twelve hours, enough to soften it and remove some of the salt. It was then broiled on a grate over live coals. During the broiling it was repeatedly basted with a condiment of olive oil, vinegar and white wine, minced garlic, and lots of black pepper. The basting was done with a long sprig of rosemary, the leaves of which had been bruised with the fingers to release the aromatic oil. The fare was humble—nothing is so lowly as salt cod—but the culinary genius of the race, plus the joyful occasion, gave it a festive blessing of a sort. The dish is well worth trying on a hot day with jugs of cold beer.

It was at one of these affairs that I first heard an appropriate culinary proverb: *Il pesce vive nell'acqua, e deve affogare nel vino.* Since fish thrives in water, it must be drowned in wine. It was Grandfather who fetched the proverb from his store of wisdom as he poured more wine into his goblet, thus suiting the meaning of a culinary dictum to his immediate purpose; for the proverb, of course, refers primarily to the use of wine in fish cookery.

II

Fish is a delicious and wholesome food. When it is properly prepared, the family will want to eat it frequently. The reason why it is in general disrepute and eaten more or less reluctantly on Friday, in a spirit of self-castigation, is that no other food is so consistently desecrated on the kitchen range. It is too often fried in indifferent grease after it has been satu-

rated in a thick batter which prevents it from assimilating even such simple and penetrating seasoning as
salt and pepper. The result is actually fish steamed in
a thick coating of fat-drenched cement.

For the sake of variety it is baked now and then
with salt, pepper, lemon, and a bit of water. The more
imaginative may add carrot, celery, onion, and perhaps an herb or two. The result is good and somewhat
more appetizing. But there are possibilities for improvement. Those who broil it with a simple seasoning
of salt, pepper, and lemon come much closer to ade-
quacy in fish cookery.

The more precious cookbooks, seeking to entice the
housewife from her unimaginative culinary routine,
revert to a crude medievalism in the richness and
complexity of some of the sauces suggested for fish.
A careful analysis of such recipes will reveal that they
are more ingenious than gastronomically sound. Here
are some of the ingredients suggested in one of the
"better" recipes for cooking a couple of pounds of
sole: onion, parsley, thyme, celery, lemon, carrot, bay
leaf, peppercorns, water, cooking wine, fish stock, milk,
grated cheese, three tablespoonfuls of flour, six tablespoonfuls of cream, and a cup of butter. Doesn't that
sound delicious? There is enough flour and butter to
make a cream sauce for half the soles in the English
Channel. Any recipe that specifies seasoning ingredients worth more than the thing to be seasoned is
suspect and has decadence written all over its face.

Actually, good fish cookery can be very simple if
we bear in mind a few basic principles. The bland
quality of nearly all fish should be relieved by an appropriately piquant condiment. That is why lemon is
so universally used on fish. Among the herbs, tarragon, thyme, and pennyroyal blend perfectly with fish.
Capers and bay leaf, too, are very good. And of course

one can never go wrong using parsley, garlic, and onion. Worcestershire, Tabasco and white wine should always be on hand when a fish dinner is being prepared. Small, soft fish, such as smelt and brook trout, while they may be cooked in many different ways, are best slightly coated with yellow corn meal and fried in good olive oil. Other oils will do, but olive oil is the best.

While it is desirable now and then to experiment with sauces—and I shall suggest some—most fish steaks and fillets are best when broiled and basted with some sharp basting liquid and brought to the table with a crisp and slightly browned surface. Fish sauces made with butter, flour, and cream smack of overrefinement and should be used sparingly. Whenever possible avoid scaly fish that has been skinned and boned. When the scales have been properly removed from a fish, especially trout, shad, salmon, and red snapper, the skin should be eaten, for it has more flavor than the fish. The oil and flavor in the skin and bones of fresh fish are indispensable in good fish cookery.

Let me illustrate what I have said above with a recipe for broiled red snapper. I created it some time ago as a sort of by-product of another dish that I was preparing at the moment. The genesis of this recipe has a further value. It shows a cook at work, experimenting with ingredients that he thoroughly understands and the quality of whose synthesis he can confidently predict.

I have said elsewhere that a cook is more interested in culinary ideas than in the slavish pursuit of this or that recipe. It is appropriate to add here that culinary ideas are best conceived while one is surveying in hunger the raw materials with which he must prepare dinner.

I had bought snapper for dinner because we all like it, and I had intended to broil it with a simple condiment of lemon, butter, and wine. I was also preparing for the same dinner a really delightful combination of chard, spinach, and turnip greens. I may as well give the recipe for the greens and then proceed with the snapper and thus adhere to the original chronology.

For five or six people wash and drain thoroughly, so they are completely dry, as much of the three greens in equal parts as you think are necessary. In the large kettle in which they are to be cooked prepare the following simple condiment: Mince to a pulp a piece of rather lean salt pork, about the size of a quarter-pound of butter. Put it in the kettle over a slow fire with a bit of olive oil or butter. When partially fried, add a small onion, a clove of garlic, and a sprig of parsley all minced very fine. Let them cook slowly for a few minutes, but do not brown. Then add two cups of ripe tomatoes, fresh or tinned. Increase the heat until the whole is cooking briskly and then simmer slowly with the kettle tightly covered for about fifteen minutes. Cut up the raw greens, throw them into the kettle, salt and pepper to taste, stir thoroughly, cover and cook until done. Stir frequently so that the sauce and the greens are well mixed and be sure they do not overcook. If you don't have this combination of greens, or if you don't like it, any one of them alone will do. So will any other leaf vegetable you may desire.

As I was mincing the salt pork, garlic, parsley, and onion, it occurred to me that this might be a fair beginning for cooking the snapper. So I minced a bit more. After the combination of ingredients was lightly fried as for the greens, with a bit of olive oil added— no tomato here—I smeared it on both sides of the slices of snapper. (The slices had been cut from the unskinned fish.) Then I placed the fish in the broiling pan—not on the rack—and set to work on a basting liquid. I had on hand lemons, capers, the ordinary kitchen sauces, bay leaf, bouillon cubes, herbs in the garden, and barrels of white wine in the cellar.

I was a little excited over what I had already done to the fish, confident that it had been a brilliant beginning. With hunger urging me on to a worthy complement, I proceeded as follows: Into a small saucepan went one cup of stock, one cup of white wine, six capers, half a dozen leaves of fresh tarragon, a teaspoonful of Worcestershire, a goodly dash of Tabasco, and the juice of one lemon. I brought the whole to a boil and then set it aside to steep for about fifteen minutes. Occasionally I crushed the capers and tarragon with a fork to release their flavor. Then I strained the liquid and scattered some minced parsley over it.

The fish, with a dash of cayenne on each slice, was placed under the preheated broiler, about four inches from the element. As it broiled I basted it frequently with the hot liquid. When one side was done I turned the slices and repeated the routine.

During the broiling the juices in the fish flow freely and mingle with the basting liquid in the pan. Midway in the process it may seem that there is an excess of liquid; but the heat considerably reduces and thickens it so that when done (about fifteen minutes on each side) the result is a rather thickish sauce. During the last few minutes I salted the fish and brushed each slice with a bit of butter. When well browned, I removed the slices to the serving platter, drained over them the sauce that had remained in the pan, and brought the whole confidently to the table. It was much too good for any wretched mortal.

Note particularly in this recipe the relative simplicity of ingredients, the sparing use of fats and oils, the essentially nippy character of the sauce, designed to heighten rather than subdue the flavor of the snapper, and the crispness of the fish when served. The two distinctive ingredients are the capers and the wine. I use the dry salted capers whose flavor is unimpaired. If these are not available, capers preserved in vinegar are a poor substitute.

The recipe exemplifies one type of sauce, probably the best basic sauce in most fish cookery, unless one has a predilection for cream, flour, butter, and their derivatives which, of course, are desirable now and then. A cook who has his own ideas is urged to try as many variations on the theme as may occur to him. Not all the ingredients listed are absolutely necessary. Perhaps thyme could be substituted for tarragon and vinegar for lemon with gratifying results. Let each cook make his own improvements and stand by his achievement. And so I pass on to fillet of shad.

This very delicious soft fish is excellent broiled, and bathed with lemon juice and white wine four or five times on each side during the broiling. A last-minute brushing with butter, salt, pepper, and a dash of cayenne are all the additional condiments needed.

For a totally different flavor and one that lifts the dish into the category of refined though simple cookery, proceed as follows: Put enough butter into a small saucepan to cover the bottom. Mince into it a clove of garlic, a green onion, a few mushrooms, and a bit of fresh tarragon and parsley. Cook very briefly, just enough to wilt down the ingredients. Stir in a scant teaspoonful of flour. Then add slowly, stirring briskly the while, half a cup of broth or bouillon and a cup of white wine that have been heated together in another pan. Cover and simmer for ten minutes.

While this sauce is simmering, cut the shad fillets

into the desired number of servings. Dust them with seasoned flour and brown them in a frying pan with a bit of olive oil. While the fish is frying, salt and pepper to taste, add a dash of cayenne, and squeeze lemon juice over each piece. When done, drain out the fat, spoon the sauce over the fish, and glaze under the broiler until golden brown.

This fish may be served with young beets and beet greens prepared in this way: Wash, drain, and cut the tops. Boil the beet roots, skin and slice them. In a spacious kettle, mince a quarter of a pound of ham. A lesser quantity of salt pork, very lean, or bacon will do. Add a spoonful of olive oil or butter and fry slowly until partially browned. Add a half-glass of wine vinegar and stir briskly over a hot fire. Put in the beets and beet greens, mix thoroughly, salt and pepper to taste, cover and cook until done. If there is too much liquid, remove the lid from the kettle and let some of it evaporate. Stir frequently to assure complete assimilation. Serve in separate dishes so that the juice will not mingle with the fish sauce. This is a superb fish dinner and it can be prepared in three-quarters of an hour.

By varying the herbs and using capers, perhaps a bit of anchovy paste and Worcestershire, other good sauces of this general nature may be made. The really essential ingredients are wine, lemon or vinegar, garlic, tarragon or some other herb akin to it, and a dash of some nippy kitchen sauce. The next sauce I suggest is especially recommended for sole, cod, trout, bass, and fresh-water eels.

For six servings of any one of these fish, mince very fine about a quarter of a pound of *prosciutto* (Italian ham, see next chapter) and fry in a bit of butter. Add a clove of garlic, a medium onion chopped very fine, and cook very slowly just short of browning. Add a small tin of tomato sauce and an equal quantity of bouillon or broth (four large ripe tomatoes, cooked and strained, may be substituted for the tomato sauce). Mince enough thyme to make a heaping table-spoonful, add to the sauce, and simmer slowly for half an hour, adding salt, pepper, and a cup of white wine during the last few minutes.

Dust the fish lightly in flour and brown it in olive oil or butter. Sprinkle it with a little salt, pepper, and lemon juice. Spoon a bit of the sauce into a baking dish large enough for the purpose and set the pieces of fish carefully on it so they do not overlap. Spill the rest of the sauce into the frying pan where the fish was browned, stir briskly so that the residual juices in the pan may be assimilated, and pour the whole over the fish. Place uncovered in a moderate oven for fifteen minutes. Serve with broccoli prepared in this way:

Wash and boil the broccoli until about half cooked. Drain, cut them in small pieces, and finish cooking in a pan with two tablespoonfuls of olive oil in which two cloves of garlic, cut in six pieces, have been fried until brown and then removed. Sprinkle with grated *Parmigiano*, the juice of half a lemon, salt and pepper, then place in the oven for just a few minutes to melt the cheese.

The fish sauce for the sole may be varied in this way: To the onion and garlic add a scant teaspoonful of flour. Then stir in a cup of broth and a cup of white wine heated together. When the sauce has attained the desired consistency, add a bit of minced chervil and tarragon, a cup of ripe olives, and simmer for twenty or thirty minutes. Pour over the browned fish and finish cooking as suggested above.

Black cod, baked or broiled, is a rich fish of rare delicacy and texture. I like it especially boiled in this way: Cut the desired quantity in rather large pieces and arrange in a deep pan. Add as many small potatoes as desired, a cup of white wine, two cloves of garlic, two tablespoonfuls of olive oil, salt and pepper. When it comes to a boil reduce the heat and cook slowly until the potatoes are done. Serve with peas, fresh or frozen, prepared as follows: Mince two green onions and two leaves of lettuce into a saucepan with enough butter to cover the bottom. Cook for a few minutes; then add the peas, salt and pepper to taste, cover, and simmer until done.

I was first introduced to baked black cod by a distinguished tailor in San Diego, California. This is the way he did it: Place in a roaster a chunk of black cod, as large as desired. Cut in very small pieces about ten green onions and throw them over and around the fish. Sprinkle with salt and pepper. Arrange all around the fish as many potatoes as needed, cut in thin round slices. Cut a lemon in rounds and skewer on the fish with toothpicks. Mince some parsley and celery and scatter freely over the whole. Salt and pepper the potatoes. Scatter over the whole a tablespoonful of olive oil and one of butter. Cover and cook in a moderate oven until the potatoes are done. It should bake from twenty to thirty minutes, with occasional benedictions of heated white wine. Once you have tried this dish you will return to it frequently. Serve it with thin slices of toasted bread rubbed with garlic, crisp celery, and plenty of wine.

Salted cod with leeks and chard is a most appropriate dinner for cold winter evenings. Soak the cod for twenty-four hours in plenty of cold water. Change the water at the end of the first twelve hours. Wash it and dry it thoroughly, drench it in flour and brown it in bacon fat. Set aside and prepare the following sauce in a deep skillet: Brown in butter a fifth of a pound of ham minced in very small pieces. For about six servings, cut four leeks in rather thin slices and simmer with the ham for a few minutes. Add one large can of tomatoes, or an equal quantity of ripe ones, which have been cooked and strained. Add one small hot pepper. Cook slowly for a half-hour and then add the cod and a cup of red wine. Cook for another hour. During the last twenty minutes, add six large leaves of chard finely shredded and a bit of fresh tarragon. Pepper to taste and add salt if necessary.

Serve it with lots of corn meal mush fried crisp, and as much red wine as you can drink without losing your dignity. This dish needs no further accompaniment. A dessert of fresh fruit and your favorite cheese would be most appropriate. Since the dish is so inexpensive, you can well afford some macaroons and a fine brandy with the after-dinner coffee.

For those who are fond of shellfish, I recommend the butter clams of the Pacific Northwest. If taken when they are about the size of walnuts, they make an excellent cocktail if prepared with plenty of lemon juice, lots of black pepper, freshly ground, and just a suggestion of some reputable cocktail sauce. When I dig them on the beaches of the San Juan Islands, I always have a lemon or two with me and eat them on the half shell. If the uninitiated can muster the necessary courage and disabuse his fancy of all irrelevance, he is invited to come along with me, and I shall be glad to open for him as many as he can eat. If he insists on having them cooked, I will oblige and tempt him in this way:

I shall carve them out of the shell, clip off the tip of the neck, and wash them properly so that there will be no trace of sand. I shall then mince into the skillet a clove of garlic, some parsley, a bit of tarragon, and wilt them slightly in a half-cup of butter. Then I shall put the clams into the skillet, stir them thoroughly in the condiment, sprinkle them generously with lemon juice and black pepper, and bake them in a hot oven for about twenty minutes. My guest, meanwhile, will be sipping a Martini, dry as dry ice. He will then sit at my table with two dozen clams on a hot plate, a half-loaf of French bread toasted and rubbed with garlic, and a pint of my best white wine. I shall be near by to see that he doesn't devour the plate.

Steamed clams are quite palatable with no other condiment than hot butter. However, you may, as I do, prefer them in this way: Place into the pan in which they are to be steamed a little less than a quarter of a pound of butter, a bay leaf crumpled, some coarsely chopped celery and parsley, and a clove of garlic. Scrub the clams thoroughly and put them in. Add the juice of one lemon and turn on the heat. The juice within the clams will supply the additional moisture needed. A dash of cayenne or a few drops of Tabasco will not be regretted. When the clams are opened—it should not require more than ten or fifteen minutes—drain the juice into little individual bowls, one for each guest. Set the bowl of clams on the center of the table and instruct your friends to dip the morsels into the liquid before stowing them away. It is not improbable that they will enjoy them.

My wife, who is really the better all-around cook, makes an excellent clam chowder with milk, bacon, herbs, and I don't know what else. I enjoy it without reservation. But I make it differently, and I regret to say that if she eats mine at all, she does so out of compassion. So we have agreed on one of those delightful one-way compromises that have resolved many a domestic impasse: *she* makes the chowder.

I suppose I ought now to give her recipe, and I would if I could be persuaded that it is really better than mine. There is a fundamental honesty on every page of this book from which I cannot be tempted to depart; so it is my recipe, good or bad, that must prevail.

For the average family, mince to a pulp a trifle less than a quarter of a pound of very lean salt pork. Fry it slowly in the kettle in which the chowder is to be made so that it does not brown too much or too quickly. Mince and add half an onion, a clove of garlic, a half teaspoonful of tarragon, a tablespoonful of parsley, and an equal amount of celery. Cook slowly for a few minutes, taking care not to brown the herbs, and then stir in two tablespoonfuls of tomato sauce and simmer lightly for ten minutes. Chop rather coarsely three or four leaves of chard and add them to the other ingredients, together with the necessary quantity of boiling water. When the chard is nearly cooked, add the clams cut in small pieces, salt and pepper to taste, and cook for about ten minutes or a little less. Serve with minced chervil or parsley, and lemon rind sprinkled over each bowl. I shall be delighted to know your honest judgment.

5

Some Culinary Preferences

THEY WERE the damndest pair that ever swore to be true to one another. He was a massive artisan, loose-jowled, grisly-bearded and sour-faced. The hair on his broad, thick chest spilled over his shirt collar and curled in ringlets under his chin. Large rheumy tears flowed constantly from his big blue eyes, down along the deep channels between the heavy cheeks and bulbous nose, and mingled with the beads of sweat on his broad upper lip. The outer, hairy surface of his enormous hands, always powdered with a layer of fine sawdust, was crisscrossed with bulging blue veins.

As he wielded the broad ax on a knotted tree trunk or pushed the plane over the tough surface of an oak timber, he mumbled vigorously and incessantly such a streak of curses that mendicant friars who passed his shop habitually made the sign of the cross and repeated their *Pater Nosters* and *Ave Marias* with unwonted fervor. And yet, those who were not intimidated by his brusque exterior and stopped at his cottage, never left empty-handed.

When he called to his wife, across the courtyard from his workshop, to fetch him the wine jug, his affectionate love call was the envy of all hen-ridden males who lacked his gall and the burly framework with which to back it up. *"Ei, brutta puttana sgan-*

196

gherata, quando me la porti quella benedetta botti-glia?" What ho! You ugly, unhinged whore, when are you going to bring me that blessed bottle?

At the sound of her darling's voice, she emerged belligerently from the kitchen door, a mountainous, shapeless mass draped in a heavy, loose, and volumi-nous woolen dress that, so far as the neighbors could tell, had not been changed in a quarter of a century. It was gathered somewhere above the navel with a knitted bright red scarf and extended to the ground. As she waddled across the yard, her heavy breasts swaying rhythmically from side to side, she chewed incessantly on pumpkin seeds—of which she had an inexhaustible supply—and looked intently and rather menacingly toward the shop. When she approached her mate, whom she dearly loved, she held out the wine jug and addressed him in language as vigorous and original as his own. *"Ecco la tua puttana, brutto bastardo pidocchioso. Bevi e affoga, porco ghiot-tone."* Here comes your whore, you ugly, louse-rid-den bastard. Drink and drown yourself, you glutton-ous swine.

As she handed him the bottle, he hoisted his heavy-booted foot in the general direction of her belly. It was a wholly futile thrust, for she had learned by experience that by stooping slightly forward and grab-bing his foot in mid-air, she could avoid his treacher-ous blow. When she had him thus helpless in her strong grip, she would grin and spit, then throw his boot to the ground and retreat, laughing like a witch. As she reached the middle of the courtyard she would turn her rear toward him, bend slightly forward, look over her shoulder and wink affectionately, as she let him have a blast so terrific that it fanned her skirt into a complete circle. Her talent for releasing such thunderclaps at will was so amazing that she was everywhere known as *La Trombona.*

In their rather unorthodox manner they lived in perfect marital bliss. Power and will were so evenly divided between them that their amorous banter never resulted in harm to either one. They exemplified perfectly, though in a rather bizarre and exaggerated manner, the type of Latin man and wife who enjoy each other most, when each is yelling at the other and threatening in most forbidding language.

Although well past middle age, they had no children and lived alone in a stone cottage adjoining our home. Eating together at the hearth enormous quantities of good food washed down by goblets of wine was their principal recreation. He was a master craftsman, particularly skilled in shaping the trunk and root structure of oak and chestnut trees into magnificent plows. For his labor he was frequently paid in hams, sausages, eggs, poultry, wine, and grain. Thus, and since they had no dependents, they could afford to live well above the level of the peasants whom he served in a hundred different ways.

If the reader will search his memory, he may likely discover that in his childhood there was some adult, outside of the home, who was his dearest friend; some kindly elder, full of affection and patience, who knew how to make children happy. In my childhood and early youth there were several, but none so dear as *La Trombona* and her mumbling husband. Frequently, in the morning, they called me in to share their breakfast of toasted bread dunked in large bowls of coffee and milk nicely sweetened with priceless sugar and spiked with *acqua vite.* Now and then they would fry me an egg or give me a slice of ham to eat with my figs and bread. He was never too busy to help me make a kite or construct a little wagon for my manuring expeditions.

Occasionally, when he delivered a finished plow, he took me with him to the country. When the donkey was hitched to the wagon, he put me in the driver's seat and let me hold the reins as he walked alongside the animal. One such expedition, to a particularly distant farmhouse, ended most tragically. The farmer had given us dinner, a load of hay, and a precious ham in payment for the plow. Because of the load and the difficult terrain, we were obliged to walk most of the way home and occasionally to give the donkey a hand over a rut or up a difficult incline. But it was late at night and I was soon tired and sleepy; so I was hoisted on top of the hay and given the responsibility of guarding the ham against possible loss as we jogged along over the uneven roadbed. I was soon sound asleep. When we arrived home about midnight, *La Trombona* was waiting for us with hot coffee and fresh bread, eager to sample the new ham. But the ham had been lost. The fury and the noise of the quarrel which ensued still ring in my ears. Although, in a way, I had been principally at fault, no harsh word was spoken to me. They abused and threatened each other until the good man, with lantern in hand, retraced his steps in search of the ham. I don't remember whether it was ever found.

The Italian ham (*prosciutto*) though excellent in itself, is a basic auxiliary in the cooking of meat, fowl, and vegetables. Hogs in Italy are fattened mostly on acorns, so that the flesh of the pork has a fine, nutty flavor, not unlike that of the peanut-fed porkers of Virginia.

Nowhere in Italy, except in some villages along the northern border, where the influence of Austrian cuisine is apparent, are pork products cured by smoking.

The unique flavor of the *prosciutto* derives from a rather simple curing process. The initial treatment is a two-week salt cure, followed by a thorough washing in a mild wine vinegar. The ham is then rubbed with a paste of minced garlic and fresh rosemary. It is then completely covered with a coating of black pepper and hung in the cellar for a year. At the end of that time the *prosciutto* is ready for the table and the kitchen. It is customarily eaten raw, cut in very thin slices parallel with the bone.

II

The unique flavor of the *prosciutto* makes it a very desirable ingredient in the preparation of certain meats, vegetables, fowl, and game birds. Here are some recipes in which its use lends the dish a characteristic flavor. If the *prosciutto* is not available, fresh Italian sausage, smoked ham, or pork links may be substituted in that order of preference.

Sweetbreads. Drop the sweetbreads into boiling water and let them simmer slowly for about five minutes. Remove and plunge immediately into cold water. When sufficiently cool, clean them of membrane, cartilage remnants, and whatever fat may be clinging to them. Cut them in pieces about the size of a walnut and salt and pepper to taste. Match each piece of sweetbread with a tiny slice of *prosciutto,* about an inch square and about one-eighth of an inch thick. Alternate the pieces of *prosciutto* and sweetbreads on skewers, and place in the broiling pan about four inches from the element. As they broil, turn them frequently and baste every two or three minutes with the following liquid:

Add to a cup of white wine, a teaspoonful of Worcestershire, two or three dashes of Tabasco, a clove of garlic, a sprig of marjoram, one of parsley, and a bit of chives, all finely minced. Bring the whole to a boil, remove from the fire, and steep for several minutes, keeping the pan tightly covered. Do the basting with a rosemary branch about six inches long, after it has been bruised by crushing between the hands to release the aromatic oils.

In twenty to thirty minutes the sweetbreads will be broiled to a golden brown. When the basting liquid is exhausted, continue the basting with the juice that has accumulated in the pan. If sausage is used, the fat should be partially fried out before the sausage is impaled on the skewers. During the broiling, the sweetbreads should be frequently turned so that they may be browned on all sides. A last-minute brushing with butter will enhance the flavor. Serve on the skewer with fresh or frozen peas prepared in this way:

Mince and fry slowly in a bit of butter a small slice of *prosciutto*. Add two green onions, a green leaf of lettuce, a sprig of parsley, and several leaves of fresh basil, all cut very fine. Wilt them thoroughly over a slow fire but do not brown. Add the peas (fresh string beans will do as well), salt and pepper to taste, stir well, and keep tightly covered until done.

The recipe for the sweetbreads may be varied by adding mushrooms and halved artichoke hearts properly alternated on the skewers. If the results achieved leave much to be desired, try this recipe:

Dust the pieces of sweetbreads with flour flavored with salt, pepper, cayenne, and paprika. Arrange them in pairs with a bit of *prosciutto* between two pieces and fasten them securely with toothpicks. Brown them slowly in butter with mushrooms cut in small pieces. Add bit by bit, stirring the while, half a cup of stock and an equal amount of white wine that have been heated together. Simmer slowly for fifteen or twenty minutes. During the last five minutes add a slice of lemon rind finely minced. Serve with mashed potatoes to which onion and parsley have been added.

Complete the meal with your favorite cooked vegetable and a bottle of the best wine available, white or red. The amount of stock and wine prescribed for this recipe is adequate for sweetbreads for four. If you are serving more than that number, add more wine and stock accordingly. For variety one may add a spoonful of tomato paste to the stock.

The results of blending meats are often pleasant and exciting. The *polpettone*, which is a huge roll made with the top round of beef, veal, and pork, will give anyone immediate status as a cook if he does it properly. Try it in this way:

Take a top round steak of beef cut about a half-inch thick. With a small paring knife, scrape a clove of garlic all over its surface. Salt and pepper lightly. Cover it with thin slices of *prosciutto*. Set the veal round over it, also cut a half-inch thick. Mince a few leaves of tarragon and a green onion or chives and scatter evenly over the veal. Salt and pepper lightly. Place the top round of pork, a half-inch thick, over the veal. Scatter over the pork a bit of minced rosemary, two minced hardboiled eggs, a half-cup of mushrooms lightly fried in butter, and half a cup of grated *Parmigiano*. Roll tightly and tie securely with strong twine. Brown the roll in olive oil and butter.

Heat a cup of white wine and a cup of good beef broth. Stir in a teaspoonful of tomato paste. Pour half the liquid into the roasting pan, set the roll in it, and place in a medium oven for an hour and a half. Use the other half of the hot liquid for frequent basting. When the meat is done, the sauce may be thickened with a bit of flour.

During the first hour keep the roasting pan covered

and turn the roll frequently. Remove the cover for the last half-hour, increase the heat, and baste frequently. When the basting liquid is exhausted, use more white wine. When the roll is about cooked, brush lightly with butter. When nicely browned, remove to the serving platter and pour over it all the sauce left in the roasting pan. Slice it as you would a rolled roast and spoon some of the sauce over each slice. If you have never blended these three meats before, you will be delighted by the color combination as well as by the flavor.

An excellent vegetable to serve with the *polpettone* is string beans. Mince a bit of *prosciutto* and fry lightly in oil or butter. Add a clove of garlic and several leaves of rosemary minced very fine. Cook gently for a few minutes, then add half a cup of stock. Shred the beans in diagonal sections, put them into the pan with the other ingredients, stir thoroughly, salt and pepper to taste, and cook until tender. Stir frequently and avoid overcooking. Give your guests plenty of red wine and French bread. A dessert of fresh peaches sliced in sweet sherry will complete a perfect dinner. If possible, the peaches should be sliced into the sherry some time in the morning and kept in the refrigerator until time to serve.

Among beef-eating Anglo-Saxons, veal is not as much in favor as it is among Europeans. Possibly one of the reasons is that the former have never bothered much about the possibilities of veal cookery. A good beefsteak needs little else than skillful broiling and a simple condiment of salt and pepper. Veal requires the pungent flavor of herbs and the less frequently used condiments in order to release its latent flavor. Here are two of my contributions to the proper appreciation of adolescent beef:

Cut the thinnest possible slice of veal round into

three-inch squares. Flatten them with a wooden mallet or the broad side of a cleaver. Scrape a little garlic on each piece of the meat. Mince to a paste equal quantities of parsley, thyme, and lemon rind. Smear a little of the paste on each square. Salt and pepper to taste. Add a dash of cayenne and sprinkle each piece with grated *Parmigiano*. Place on top of each square a very thin slice of *prosciutto* equal in size to the veal. Roll and fasten with toothpicks. Brown the little rolls in oil and butter. Remove and set to one side.

In the skillet in which the rolls were browned, add two green onions, six capers, and a little bit of tarragon finely minced. Fry lightly and add a cup of mushrooms cut in pieces. Cook slowly for a few minutes, then stir in half a teaspoonful of flour. Stir in slowly one cup of heated stock. Return the veal rolls to the skillet and add two tablespoonfuls of cream. Cover and simmer slowly for ten minutes. Add half a glass of dry sherry and cook for ten minutes longer. Serve with carrots sliced thin and cooked in parsley and butter. Wine? Of course. French bread? Certainly. Potatoes? If you must. Dessert? Fresh fruit followed by coffee and a good brandy. When I served this dinner to a group of dear friends, one of them flattered me with this simple testimonial: "Aren't you all glad you didn't die yesterday?"

Next time you see some fine veal chops with a slice of the kidney attached, cook them in this way: Smear each of them with a bit of minced rosemary. Brown slowly in oil and butter. Remove and set aside. Into the skillet in which they were browned, place a dozen or so small onions the size of a cherry. Brown them with a clove of garlic and a few leaves of *oregano* finely minced. Stir in a teaspoonful of flour. Add a cup of white wine and a cup of stock heated together.

Cook for a few minutes and then remove into a bowl. Return the chops to the skillet, pour the contents of the bowl over them, cover, and simmer for twenty minutes. Serve with zucchini cut in long thin slices, dipped in egg batter and flour and French fried.

The above recipe may be varied in this way: Cut veal steak or cutlets in small pieces and brown them in fresh bacon fat. Remove and set aside. Mince into the skillet two green onions, a clove of garlic, a sprig of marjoram, and two leaves of fresh sage. Fry lightly add a teaspoonful of flour, and stir until golden brown. Add a cup of stock heated and a teaspoonful of tomato paste. Blanch as many fresh artichoke hearts as will fit into the skillet and add to the sauce. Cook for a few minutes, salt and pepper to taste, and then remove the entire contents of the skillet into the convenient bowl. Return the meat to the skillet, salt and pepper, and pour over it the artichokes and the sauce. Add a cup of white wine and simmer for twenty minutes. Serve with quantities of radishes, green onions, and celery. The meat and the artichokes may be served over a cup of boiled rice for each guest. Pears and Philadelphia cream cheese will be a good dessert.

When the garden yields its abundance of fresh vegetables and the hens drop their eggs with reckless abandon, the entire family will enjoy an occasional *frittata*. Fry a slice of *prosciutto*, cut in very small bits. If that is not available, use pork links, Italian sausage, bacon, or ordinary ham. If sausages are used care should be taken to drain off most of the grease. This is best done by broiling them. Then they may be cut in small pieces and placed in the skillet where the *frittata* is to be made.

Cut very fine a dozen green onions, two leaves of chard, three or four sprigs of parsley, six leaves of

fresh basil, three medium zucchini, and several zucchini blossoms. Put all in the skillet over the *prosciutto*
or sausage, salt and pepper to taste, cover and cook
slowly until the vegetables are about done. Beat six
eggs (for six servings) and pour over the vegetables.
Cook slowly for three or four minutes, probing occasionally with a fork that the egg may run to the bottom of the skillet. To prevent sticking, run a knife
around the edge of the skillet. Sprinkle a cup of grated
Parmigiano or *Romano* over the top and place the
skillet under the broiler. As it begins to brown, brush
lightly with butter. When golden brown bring the
frittata to the table and cut in wedges as you would a
pie. Serve with French fried potatoes and good bread.

III

As I have suggested above, a beefsteak should be
broiled. In buying a steak don't be penny-wise and
pound-foolish. Avoid the bony steaks, such as T-bone
and porterhouse. There is too much waste in such
cuts. The best buys are top sirloin (New York cut)
and top round, if your butcher will assure you that
it is tender. I have always found that a tender top
round has more flavor than any other cut.

Now for the broiling. Scrape garlic on both sides
of the steak. Salt and pepper to taste. The traditional
advice is not to salt a steak until it is done since, we
are told, salt induces the juice to run out of the meat.
If this be true, your compensation is in the added
flavor produced by cooking the salt and pepper into
the meat. In any case, the juice drips into the broiling
pan and may be poured over the steak as it broils
and when it is served. Place the steak in a very hot
broiler about two inches away from the element. To

make certain it is cooked to the degree which pleases you most, it is wise to probe into it with a fork occasionally to see what is going on inside. If you like Worcestershire on your steak, sprinkle it on during the broiling.

What to serve with a steak? The reader is entitled to my best advice, and here it is: Good bread, good wine, a good salad, celery, radishes, green onions, and French fried or pan broiled potatoes. Avoid cooked vegetables. Why? Because you had them yesterday and you may have them again tomorrow.

What is a good salad for a steak? A good salad is a *simple* salad, made with slightly bitterish greens. The present vogue reflects a misplaced recklessness. There are too many ingredients, minced and sliced and then bathed in a dressing that is little else than a hodgepodge of condiments. Such salads are a violent (and, I should say, salutary) reaction to sliced tomato and lettuce hearts covered with mayonnaise. But while we strive for improvement let's keep our heads.

Try these simple salads with your next steak. In the early spring, fill your bowl with tender dandelion shoots. With the first spring crop from the garden, fill your bowl with leaf lettuce and romaine, or the first tender leaves of chicory. In the fall, fill the bowl with endive or escarole. Add to all of them a bit of minced parsley and watercress.

And what about the dressing? This is absolutely the best: herb-flavored vinegar, good olive oil, salt, pepper, and toasted bread rubbed with garlic and cut in pieces as for croutons. If you want a fine-flavored vinegar, make it in this way: Stuff loosely a quart jar with fresh tarragon and basil leaves. Add two hot chile peppers and two crushed cloves of garlic. Fill the quart with wine vinegar, seal tightly, and let it stand for ten days or two weeks. Shake the jar violently every two or three days. Then strain and add enough wine vinegar to make three pints. The result will be something precious.

In making the salad, let your taste rather than arbitrary measurements be your guide. Put the garlic-flavored croutons in the bottom of the bowl. Add the salad greens. Sprinkle with salt and pepper, olive oil and vinegar in about equal quantities. Be rather miserly at first. Give the salad a preliminary tossing and then taste it. Add more of whatever else it needs. Continue the process until your taste is satisfied. If there are other people around, call for a consultation. You will soon learn how to do it independently and without tasting, if that is a desirable objective. But if you always taste as you go along, you will always be certain of results.

To grace the steak and salad, prepare your potatoes in this way. Cut them in quarters and drop them into heated fat or olive oil in a shallow cookie sheet. Not too much fat—just enough to cover the bottom of the pan. Roll the potatoes in the oil until they are completely drenched. Throw in four or five sprigs of fresh sage, several cloves of garlic, salt and pepper to taste, and cook quickly in a very hot oven. Turn them once so that they will brown on both sides.

There are dinners more elaborate and expensive to be sure but none could be more pleasant and more wholesome, especially when the wine and bread are both of fine quality. For those who prefer a sauce over the steak, I suggest the following: Mince and fry in butter a small onion and a clove of garlic. Add as many cut mushrooms as you desire. Stir in a teaspoonful of flour. Add a cup of stock, a teaspoonful of Worcestershire, a dash of Tabasco, and two tablespoonfuls of dry sherry. Simmer for ten minutes and spread over the steak during the last few minutes of broiling.

All pork meat should be well cooked. The herb that blends most satisfactorily with pork is fresh sage. Pork steak and chops, whether broiled or fried, should be cut rather thin. When served they should be golden brown and somewhat crisp. Before putting them into the broiler or the frying pan, smear them well with garlic and minced sage. If broiled, baste them frequently with the juice that drips into the broiler pan.

Young turnips and turnip greens are an excellent vegetable to serve with fried pork. When the steak or chops have been browned, remove them from the skillet. Fry in the meat juice a clove of garlic, a small onion, and half a chile pepper crushed or powdered. Add half a cup of tomatoes and simmer for twenty minutes.

Blanch the turnips and greens for four minutes. Drain well, cut them fine, and put them into the sauce. Stir well and finish cooking over a slow fire. During the last few minutes, arrange the meat over the greens and cover until the meat is hot all through. Serve with bread, red wine, and baked potatoes.

Prepare a roast of pork in this way. Several hours before putting it into the oven, salt and pepper it thoroughly. Cut several holes in the roast and force into each of them pepper and salt, a sliver of garlic, and two leaves of fresh sage. If convenient, let it stand overnight. Roast it in an open roaster and baste it frequently with its own juice. During the last hour, surround it with as many small potatoes as you need. Salt and pepper them well and turn them frequently so that when the roast is done the potatoes will be crisp and brown. A salad of romaine, escarole, or dandelion shoots will provide the perfect vegetable.

In roasting veal and lamb, follow the above procedure and use fresh rosemary and thyme instead of sage. Baste the lamb with a mild, flavored vinegar and the veal with a good white wine.

If you enjoy broiled spareribs try this recipe: Mince to a fine paste a clove of garlic, a sprig of rosemary, three or four leaves of sage, and a small onion. Add a cup of red wine, a tablespoonful of olive oil, half a teaspoonful of Tabasco, and two tablespoonfuls of chile sauce. Bring the ingredients to a boil and steep for ten minutes. Bathe the ribs in this sauce, salt and pepper them well, and let them stand for several hours. Broil them slowly about five inches away from the element. Baste them frequently with the remaining sauce and with the juice that drips into the pan. Serve with celery and hearts of savoy cabbage.

A good roast of beef is best with the simplest possible condiment. Small cloves of garlic pierced deep into the meat, salt and pepper, are all that is necessary. This procedure may be varied by washing the roast in red wine and then basting it frequently with the same wine heated to the boiling point.

An excellent lamb and lamb kidney stew is an example of what can be done with inexpensive meat. Have the butcher cut two lamb shanks into small pieces. Brown them and then let them simmer in a cup of wine for about an hour. Meanwhile, cover twelve lamb kidneys with water, add three tablespoonfuls of wine vinegar, bring them to a boil, take them from the fire, and let them steep for five minutes. Plunge them into cold water, remove the surrounding membrane, slice them, and add to the shanks when the latter have simmered a full hour. Mince a small onion and a clove of garlic, add them to the kidneys and shanks, and cook slowly for a few minutes. Salt and pepper to taste.

To a cup of stock add a bay leaf, a sprig of rosemary, the juice of one lemon, and a teaspoonful of tomato paste. Bring to a boil and steep for fifteen minutes. Strain and add to the meat and the kidneys. Simmer slowly until done. Remove the cover during the last ten minutes to reduce the sauce. Serve with boiled rice and your favorite cooked vegetable.

I once prepared a rather elaborate dinner for a group of people about whom, gastronomically speaking, I was a little uncertain. While shopping at the meat market, I saw some excellent tripe that I could not resist buying—for myself. During the dinner hour I explained to my guests that I had prepared some tripe for myself and invited them to taste it. No one in the group had ever eaten it before. Their response was amazing. I was obliged to forego the tripe and to eat the elaborate fare I had prepared for my guests. These friends have since become veteran tripe-eaters at my table.

There is no waste in tripe, so figure on a little better than half a pound per person. Wash it thoroughly and remove the globules of fat that adhere to the inner walls. Slice it in longitudinal strips about a quarter of an inch wide. Boil it for about fifteen minutes in enough water to cover. Wash it again in cold water and drain thoroughly.

In a deep, spacious skillet, prepare the following sauce for five pounds of tripe: Cover the bottom of the pan with good olive oil. Mince thoroughly the following ingredients: an onion, two cloves of garlic, a sprig of parsley, three sprigs of thyme, two strips of lemon rind, half a stalk of celery, a quarter of a medium carrot, and six capers. The capers are very important and should be the dry, salted variety. Fry these minced ingredients very lightly (do not brown) in the oil, then add a large can of tomatoes. Add salt, pepper, cayenne, and a dash or two of allspice. Simmer for ten or fifteen minutes, then add the tripe and cook slowly for two hours. At the end of two hours add a cup of grated *Romano,* a cup of bread crumbs, and two cups of white wine. Stir thoroughly and simmer slowly for another half-hour. Serve with boiled rice, French bread, and good wine.

At our home a tripe feed is a tripe feed, and we serve nothing else with it. Occasionally we warm up to the meal with celery, lettuce, radishes, olives, tuna, green onions, and anchovies, served with a Martini or two at the table. A group of friends, who ask for it periodically, eat it with great relish and expect nothing else except the after-dinner coffee and brandy.

6

Chicken and
Other Small Fry

ON A FRIDAY afternoon in early June, 1917, Mr. Peter Donovan appeared before the seventh grade class of which I was a rather bewildered member, to lecture on the agricultural wonders of The Valley that he had done so much to exploit, so the teacher had informed us, in the interest of the general welfare. He spoke eloquently of the large berries, the contented cows, the mammoth potatoes, and of snow-white chickens who dutifully laid an egg a day. At the conclusion of the lecture he announced that arrangements had been made for our class to visit The Valley on the following Monday.

I remember the difficulty that I had in trying to make Father understand the educational relevance of berries, potatoes, chickens, and cows—an undertaking that taxed my eloquence no little, since I was (and still am) myself in considerable doubt on the matter. Somewhat reluctantly, I was given permission to go; and what I saw, although it contributed nothing to my desire to account for the difference in pronunciation between *dough* and *trough,* filled me with a sense of wonder and security.

The food production of The Valley could be described only in language now used with such vulgar disregard for propriety by Hollywood publicity agents.

I understood then what the teacher had meant when she said that the dairy cows in The Valley, lined up nose to tail, would stretch across the "wide bosom" of the American continent, and that the yearly yield of cabbage was enough to dam the Mississippi at its widest point. As this was only one of several dozen such valleys in America, a lad who had come here in search of food could certainly face the future with confidence. Subsequent crises have made necessary a re-examination of that initial faith.

The cows were indeed contented, as they munched casually on hay and grain products in large, airy barns, white and impeccably clean. Thousands of gallons of milk, in glistening cans, were stacked in the milkhouse. A drayman, we were told, would soon haul them to the dairy where the milk would undergo the blessings of pasteurization. The berry vines, neatly trellised and well cultivated, were bent with fruit reddening in the late spring sun.

But by all odds the most amazing sight was what was described as "the largest poultry farm" in The Valley. There were ten thousand white Leghorns in the flock, housed in a series of white, clean, and well-ventilated coops that might well have been taken as models for metropolitan slum clearance. The food was distributed in clean troughs so arranged that the chickens might not, in their casual manner, use them for more intimate purposes. The central heating plant maintained an even temperature calculated to keep Miss Leghorn's mind on her work—an egg a day. The lighting system was the most fraudulent device that man has ever perpetrated on his less intelligent underlings. In the model chicken coop it was perpetual day, and the poor hens literally wore themselves out to keep up the pretense. Betty MacDonald, could she ever be persuaded to view such an arrangement, would drool with nostalgia for the good old days.

Our guide told us with pride that by the shrewd manipulation of heat, light, and diet, the possibilities of egg production per hen per year were literally unlimited. How long the hen would survive the deception he saw no reason to explain. Nor did he explain what was immediately apparent to me: the total absence of roosters among the white and pert feathery maidens. The reason I learned much later. It reduces itself to this: On the American assembly line, there is no room for sentiment.

I was still very much an immigrant and had never wandered beyond the confines of the little lumbering town into which we had settled; so the visit to The Valley, which seemed hundreds of miles away, was my first intimate glimpse of large-scale America. The impression is still vivid in my mind. It is an impression of quantity and uniformity. The animals were all large and sleek and well fed; the extensive acres were set out in symmetrical patterns of fruit trees and vegetables; the ten thousand chickens were all white, all clean, all of a size.

Many years later I was able to appreciate fully the words of the English critic and political economist, the late G. Lowes Dickinson: "How large are the American fruits! How tall the trees! How immense the oysters!" How ingenious her people! How resourceful! And how generous, in a large, almost reckless way!

When we had completed the tour of inspection, our guide announced that he had a surprise for us: we were to be the dinner guests of the local Four H Club in the basement of the Methodist church. With shouts of joy and glowing with anticipation, we scampered out of the poultry enclosure and went to the church.

After we had sung the first verse of *America* and

were seated at a long table in that rather bleak setting, our hosts came merrily in, bearing platters of fried chicken and bowls of fresh peas. There were also homemade biscuits and jars of honey—another of The Valley's typical products. The dessert was huge wedges of apple pie topped with ice cream.

The dinner was in the best agrarian tradition—honest, simple, tasty, and in amazing abundance. It reflected perfectly the opulence of that farming community and the generosity of a people who can give of their goods with a liberal hand and never miss what they have given away.

At the conclusion of the dinner we sang a hymn—something about "count your blessings"—and then we were ushered out. As we left that church, whose colors I was later to bear in athletic combats, I could not help observing in sad bewilderment the platters of chicken that remained, the partially eaten pieces on every plate, and the fringes of piecrust of which, no doubt, some grandmother was so justly proud. "*Questa é l'America*," I murmured, and went home to tell an expectant family how far I had advanced my education.

II

A visitor unacquainted with our eating habits would soon discover that chicken is festive fare. Suburban areas and the highways across the continent are dotted with "Chicken Dinner" places. It is a safe guess that three-fourths of the people who eat out on Sundays and holidays habitually "take the chicken dinner." It is a safe, conservative choice and frequently a good one.

In a country so devoted to fowl, one might reasonably expect to find chicken cookery of some distinction. The curse of plenty, however, has discouraged experimentation in fowl cookery, in which Americans, particularly in the southern states, have made such a brilliant beginning. American chicken is roasted, fried, or stewed—and fried much more frequently than roasted or stewed. The roast is indifferent; the fry is superb. The best American fried chicken is the best fried chicken available anywhere. The Italians fry chicken with such ineptitude as is wholly unexplainable in a people who have contributed so much to good cooking. They coat it with a thick batter and fry it crisp in deep fat. What is more unimaginative, unless it be breaded veal cutlets at the Greasy Spoon?

This method of desecrating chicken is also followed in many of the more "popular" native chicken dinner joints that dot the American landscape. Frequently old hens are used, steamed in huge pressure cookers, and then given the batter and grease treatment. But in the more exclusive places, where the genuinely American tradition prevails, the fowl is choice and the results leave little to be desired. The jointed chicken is dusted with flour flavored with salt, pepper, and paprika. It is then browned in good fat, preferably butter. The excess fat is drained from the pan, a cup of cream is added, and the chicken simmered until bones and flesh begin to part. The result is juicy, succulent morsels—a real achievement in fowl cookery and a distinct contribution to good living.

When the American insists on serving with it corn on the cob and hot biscuits with honey, I part company with him, as indeed I avoid anyone who serves jams and jellies with meat. He belongs in the camp of King Arthur, whose favorite food was plum and fat. I prefer my fried chicken with an abundance of raw, crisp vegetables, good bread, and a modest white wine. If a better wine is available, I have no trouble setting modesty aside.

I can suggest a variation on the American recipe, though scarcely an improvement. When the chicken is frying throw in a few sprigs of chervil or tarragon, and substitute very dry sherry or sauterne for the cream.

In roasting chicken, capon, pheasant, and turkey, avoid water, avoid steaming, and learn the use of herbs. Make certain that the fowl is young. Use, if possible, heavy red fryers for roasting, and prepare the bird for the oven a day or several hours before it is to be roasted. Wash and dry it well, salt it and pepper it thoroughly inside and out. Then rub it well with one of the following marinades:

Mince very fine two cloves of garlic, a tablespoonful of parsley, one of celery, half of tarragon, and one green onion. Mix in a bowl with two tablespoonfuls of tarragon vinegar and one of olive oil. Marinade number two: Mince two cloves of garlic, a green onion, a tablespoonful of fresh sage and rosemary mixed. Mix in oil and vinegar as suggested above. Marinade number three: Two cloves of garlic, a green onion, a tablespoonful of parsley, one of thyme and marjoram mixed, two tablespoonfuls of olive oil, and a cup of white wine.

When the bird has been rubbed with the marinade, set it aside in a bowl. Before placing it in the oven, fasten around it three strips of fat *prosciutto* or bacon. Preheat the oven and roast at three hundred degrees. Leave the roaster uncovered and baste the bird frequently with heated white wine. If you plan to serve potatoes, roast them with the bird during the last hour. If the bird is a fryer and the potatoes are whole and about medium size, they should be placed in the oven at the same time as the bird. The best vegetable to serve with roast fowl is your favorite green vegetable salad.

When it is not expedient to make the marinades, the best alternative is to stuff the bird with any one of the combination of herbs suggested above. A slightly greater quantity of each should be used and some sprigs should be tucked under the wings and between the thighs and the body.

For festive occasions you may want a stuffing for the bird. Stuffings such as chestnut, oysters, bread, sage, and celery are a dime a dozen. I suggest one that is likely to be more appreciated than the bird in whose visceral cavity it receives its final benediction. For an ordinary chicken, proceed as follows:

Mince and fry very lightly in butter and over a slow fire, these ingredients: a clove of garlic, a green onion, a tablespoonful of tarragon and parsley mixed, one of celery, and three capers. Fry half a pound of ground lean beef and pork mixed. Drain off the fat. Add the herbs and mix thoroughly. Add two tablespoonfuls of minced cooked spinach, a bit of broth to moisten the mixture, and cook slowly for a few minutes. Mix in half a cup of bread crumbs and an equal quantity of grated *Parmigiano*. Stuff the bird at both ends and sew the incision with needle and thread. For stuffing the neck and the craw cavity, slit the skin the full length of the neck and remove the bony inner core where it joins the back. For the larger birds, such as turkey and capon or goose, increase the amount of each ingredient accordingly.

This is an excellent stuffing for all domestic fowl. It also has other uses. If you want to achieve a certain elegance next time you serve fried chicken, heap it in a large green platter and surround it with stuffed tomatoes and zucchini.

The above stuffing, with minor changes, will prove

excellent for the purpose. After the herb ingredients have been cooked in butter for a little while, add to them, finely minced, half the substance scooped out of the tomatoes and zucchini. Cook slowly for ten minutes and then proceed as outlined above. Add an extra half-cup of *Parmigiano* and bread crumbs. Select the smaller zucchini and firm, partially ripe tomatoes. Salt and pepper to taste before stuffing them and bake in a slow oven. If you do this well and time your dinner carefully, your next problem will be to live up to your reputation.

The secret of superior broiling is in the basting liquid and in keeping the meat far enough away from the element to prevent scorching and superficial cooking. Unlike steak, fowl should cook slowly in the broiler. For squab, broilers, and very young rabbit, I suggest the following basting liquid. It may be varied according to the taste and gastronomic instincts of the cook. For a two-pound broiler, mince to a fine paste a clove of garlic, a sprig of parsley, and a dozen or so leaves of fresh tarragon. Cook them for a few minutes in two tablespoonfuls of butter. Add two tablespoonfuls of tarragon vinegar, two of white wine, and half a cup of broth. Heat but do not boil.

Cut the chicken or squab into as many pieces as you wish; arrange them in the broiling pan and salt and pepper to taste. Preheat the broiler and adjust the pan about five inches away from the element. Brush frequently with the basting liquid and turn the pieces as many times as necessary to brown them on both sides. Rabbit should marinate for ten or twelve hours, longer if possible, in white wine or mild wine vinegar before broiling.

Artichokes and green salad are excellent vegetable accompaniments to the broiled fowl. If artichokes supplement the salad, a half for one serving will be enough. Instead of dipping the boiled artichoke in melted butter, you may enjoy a simple dressing made in this way: To equal quantities of olive oil and lemon juice or vinegar, add salt, pepper, a dash of Tabasco, and a teaspoonful of Worcestershire. Shake vigorously in a small bottle or jar and pour into small individual bowls, one for each guest. You will also discover a new delight in celery, green onions, radishes, leeks, and escarole leaves dipped in this piquant dressing.

A man who loves good food has a way of making it gravitate toward his kitchen. Squabs are difficult to find, but I have found a good farmer who keeps me provided. Friends in scattered parts of the country occasionally send me choice game birds, such as quail, snipe, and other small fry. There is a recipe for preparing these diminutive delicacies which I have never been tempted to vary. I learned it from my father, who was a resourceful hunter. It is as completely satisfying as any recipe could be. Cut these little fellows into very small pieces, salt and pepper them well, and arrange them on small skewers in this way: A piece of bird, a leaf of fresh sage, a piece of *prosciutto* or ham an inch square and cut rather thin, a piece of stale bread an inch square, rubbed with garlic, and a mushroom. Repeat until the skewer is full. Drench each skewer in good olive oil, arrange them in a shallow pan, and place in a very hot oven. Brush frequently with butter until nicely browned. If you are using six-inch skewers and invite me to dinner, I warn you that I shall not settle for less than half a dozen. I promise to bring my own bread, my own wine, and a chicory salad.

I have eaten a variety of food in the past twenty years and I have never hesitated to taste unfamiliar fare recommended by people of discriminating palate. But no dish has pleased me more nor left me so completely satisfied as the one described above. The only consideration in its disfavor is that for centuries small fry thus broiled have nourished the pride and the palpitating eloquence of Italian aristocrats. To the last man those nostalgic Ciceronians who found Mussolini so convenient a buffer against the increasing discontent of the people, have felt a strong gastronomic bias for larks, figpeckers, and swallows. To my everlasting shame I was once a barefoot urchin who occasionally catered to their gluttonous needs.

III

In the chapter on the garden I discussed at some length the cardoon, a vegetable which all my friends have eaten with enthusiastic avidity. It is time to say something about its preparation for the table.

The bleached, tender inner stalks of the cardoon are the edible portion. They are cleaned like celery, cut into pieces about three inches long, and given a brief preliminary scalding in salted water. When drained they may be dipped in a light batter and French fried, or prepared in this way:

For six servings, mince to a pulp about a fifth of a pound of lean salt pork and fry until golden brown. If there is too much fat drain some of it off. Add to the salt pork a large clove of garlic, a medium onion, three sprigs of parsley, and a sprig of marjoram finely minced. Cook slowly for one minute and add a cup of tomatoes and a cup of stock. Simmer for fifteen minutes and add the pieces of scalded cardoon. Cover tightly, cook until tender, and salt and pepper to taste. Stir frequently to assure complete assimilation. A few minutes before serving, stir in half a cup of *Parmigiano* and a half a cup of bread crumbs. Serve with chicken prepared in this way:

Cut as for frying a three- or four-pound fryer. Dust the pieces with flour, salt, and pepper, and brown them in butter or olive oil. Remove the chicken and set aside. Cut in halves half a pound of mushrooms and fry slowly in the pan where the chicken was browned. Mince two cloves of garlic, a green onion, a small sprig of rosemary, and a sprig of thyme. Cook for one minute with the mushrooms. Stir in half a teaspoonful of flour and add a cup of heated stock. Return the chicken to the pan and cook for fifteen minutes. Add a cup of white wine and finish cooking. Stir frequently and leave the pan uncovered if the sauce seems too thin. Give the dish whatever name suits your fancy and serve only to the most deserving guests.

If cardoons are not available, serve artichokes prepared after this fashion: Trim and plunge the artichokes into boiling salted water (enough to cover) to which has been added the juice of one lemon. Boil for three minutes and drain. For six artichokes, mince and fry slowly a quarter of a pound of *prosciutto* or ham. Add a clove of garlic, a green onion, and two small sprigs of marjoram finely minced, and fry slowly for another minute. Add half a cup of stock and simmer for five minutes. Salt and pepper to taste, stir in two tablespoonfuls of *Parmigiano,* and remove from the fire. Stuff each of the artichokes with some of this mixture and set them in a baking dish into which you have placed two tablespoonfuls of butter, half a cup of stock, a tablespoonful of tomato paste, and the juice of half a lemon. Bake in a medium oven until tender, basting frequently with the juice in the bottom of the pan.

Chicken and artichokes may be cooked together for a casserole dish of considerable merit. Cut and brown a heavy fryer in butter and olive oil. Remove the chicken and mince into the pan a large clove of garlic and a very small onion. When partially brown, mix in half a teaspoonful of flour. Add a cup of hot stock with a tablespoonful of tomato paste. Bring to a boil and add a mixed tablespoonful of parsley and rosemary. Cook for a few minutes, then add six raw artichokes, trimmed and halved. Set the chicken on top of the artichokes, salt and pepper to taste; add a cup of white wine, cover, and place in a slow oven. Bake until done.

One day there were six people for dinner. In the refrigerator there were four Italian sausages and a light, scrawny fryer. In the garden were string beans, artichokes, zucchini, carrots, beets, peas, and several other vegetables. The cellar, as usual, was well stocked and bread was in abundance. What could be done? This was done:

The chicken and the sausages were cut into pieces and browned in our very large, deep skillet. The meat was removed, and into the skillet went two cloves of garlic, two green onions, three sprigs of parsley, and six leaves of fresh basil minced. When cooked for one minute, a cup of hot water with the juice of one lemon and two tablespoonfuls of tomato paste were added. This was stirred and simmered for a few minutes. Then were added three artichokes trimmed and halved and four cups of string beans cut into small pieces. These were cooked for five minutes, then three small zucchini cut in two were added. After salting and peppering to taste, the meat was placed on top of the vegetables, a cup of white wine was sprinkled over the whole, the skillet was covered and set in a slow oven for twenty minutes or until well done. The guests were happy and satisfied. We all agreed that what gave the dish its exquisite taste was the blending of wine, lemon juice, and the flavor of the artichokes.

The war taught the American people that some animal flesh they had formerly eschewed can be relished. Horse meat is being sold in increasing quantities. Rabbits are now eaten more frequently and by more people than they were before the war. The high price asked for them attests their growing popularity. If you have never eaten rabbit, let me suggest a casserole dish that may make you an enthusiastic convert.

Cut the rabbit and soak it in enough white wine to cover for twenty-four hours. Dry it thoroughly, dust it with flavored flour, and brown it in a small quantity of olive oil and butter. Remove the meat and brown in the same fat six small carrots, a cup of mushrooms, and six small onions. Remove and set aside with the meat. Mince into the same pan a clove of garlic, two sprigs of parsley, three of marjoram, and two slices of lemon peel cut the full length of the lemon. Simmer for a minute, then add a teaspoonful of flour and stir briskly until the whole has been absorbed. Heat a cup of dry sherry and one of stock and stir slowly. Salt and pepper to taste, add a dash of cayenne, and pour into an appropriate casserole. Put in the rabbit, the mushrooms, the carrots, and the onions and stir so that all is bathed in the sauce. Cover and set in a slow oven for about forty-five minutes. Serve with boiled, buttered rice, sprinkled generously with *Parmigiano*. If this does not increase your respect for rabbit, you may safely conclude that you simply do not like it.

Polenta and chicken or rabbit stew is now traditional fare in our home. Our friends expect it as regularly as they expect tripe. We serve it during the bleak winter months because it is a dish that warms the body more than any other known to me. Furthermore, stirring the *polenta* requires about an hour over a hot stove—a task to be avoided during the warmer months.

The *polenta* dinner is always an exciting occasion—for the guests because they love it, and for me because it is a symbol of what America means to the immigrant. *Polenta* in itself is more common peasant fare than beans, and I have dealt elsewhere in this book with this monotonous ingredient in the Italian peasant's diet. The reason why it is now a symbol of America's meaning to the immigrant is that he eats it when he desires it and serves it with such elegant accompaniment as chicken or rabbit stew instead of the stinking pilchard. Thus it has become the perfect example of what I have called naturalized Italian cuisine. There is a further symbolism in the dish if one cares to search for it.

We have served many *polenta* dinners in our home, but the occasion I remember most vividly is the first time we served it to the entire family of the distinguished American composer George Frederick McKay. George is the most completely unprejudiced individual I have ever known. In all the arts he has a wholesome and inexhaustible zest for everything that is fundamentally good, be it old or new, foreign or domestic. His catholicity of taste, so admirably shared by his intelligent wife, he has unobtrusively communicated to as fine a brood of children as ever turned an American home into a circus. Though we seldom include children in our dinner parties, we occasionally like to feed the McKay kids because their reactions are enthusiastic, genuinely appreciative, and inspired by a wholesome curiosity. As they had been nourished on traditional American cuisine, they came to the *polenta* dinner wholly unprepared; and yet they fell to with the inspired relish of young gourmets. Their intelligent curiosity about the wine left little doubt that two or three of them will some day have a well-stocked cellar.

Making *polenta* is a bit of hard work, and so far as I know there are no short cuts. Use a coarse grind of yellow corn meal and a heavy kettle. If you fill it half full of water it will be three-quarters full of *polenta* when the cooking is completed. With this clue as your guide, use your own judgment as to the amount. When the water boils, salt it and throw in a quarter of a pound of butter. The butter will prevent spurting and lumping as you add the corn meal. This must be added in driblets while you stir constantly. The best implement for stirring is a round stick about an inch in diameter and two feet long. As the *polenta* hardens, the stirring will become increasingly diffi‧cult, so that if you lack the skill and the strength, you may need someone to hold the kettle while you wield the stirring rod with both hands. You have added enough corn meal when the mixture is hard enough so that the stick will stand upright in it. At the first sign of thickening, add no more meal until more seems necessary. So proceed cautiously. When it has cooked an hour, with more or less constant stirring, pour it out on a large mincing board covered with a napkin. When partially cooled, slice it, put two slices on each dish, and cover them with chicken or rabbit stew.

The chief ingredients in the stew, besides the meat, are the mushrooms, a reckless synthesis of herbs, tomato, black olives, and wine. Whether you use chicken or rabbit, the recipe is the same, remembering, of course, that the rabbit, especially an old one, should be soaked in wine or a very mild wine vinegar for twenty-four hours.

Choose an older animal; cut him in small pieces and brown them. Salt and pepper to taste, add a large can of tomatoes, a cup of stock, and let the whole simmer until nearly done. During the last half-hour add a generous cup of red wine, two cups of black olives and the following condiment:

Mince six capers and enough parsley, rosemary, thyme, and sage to make a teaspoonful of each. Brown two cups of mushrooms in butter with two cloves of garlic and an onion chopped fine. Add the herbs and cook a minute longer. Add the whole to the stew, stir well, and complete the cooking. Remember that the herbs should cook no longer than about half an hour; so time the processes accordingly.

When we serve *polenta* we serve nothing else except a good Martini (note the singular) and after-dinner coffee and brandy. This arbitary limitation is imposed out of deference to the humble origins of the dish. The table, of course, groans under bottles of choice red wine. But my penurious past, in so many ways responsible for my deep appreciation of the abundant present, I can never wholly forget.

CONCLUSION

Toward Humane Living

AMERICA!

"Land of coal and iron! land of gold! land of cotton, sugar, rice! Land of wheat, beef, pork! land of wool and hemp! land of the apple and the grape! Land of the pastoral plains, the grass-fields of the world. . . ."

Since Walt Whitman sounded his barbaric yawp over the rooftops of the world, the American land-scape has undergone considerable change. The pas-toral plains have been impoverished; many of the forests have been denuded; much of the subterranean treasure has been wastefully extracted. The builders of the nation, bold and reckless and impatient, have indeed used the body of America a little irreverently.

And yet, in an exhausted world, America remains the land of plenty. It is no exaggeration to say that the agricultural possibilities are relatively unlimited; while technological discoveries may postpone indefi-nitely the exhaustion of materials basic in the nation's economy. From every possible point of view, the op-portunities yet latent in these blessed states are the envy of the less fortunate millions of the earth. An immediate and urgent problem for the American of today is how to use them toward humane living.

Needless to say, the problem is not a simple one, and the suggestions that might be made are many and

229

varied. I have deliberately limited myself to exploring the significance of bread and wine, and the activities and attitudes that they imply, as constituents in humane living, partly because they are of basic importance, and partly because they are so frequently neglected. Because of an abiding conviction that the life of the immigrant can be fundamentally instructive to his American fellows, I have chosen to write from the detached point of view of one of them who has tried to absorb the best in the culture of America without losing what is valuable in his own. This conviction I have felt with such compelling honesty that the temptation to go beyond the limited theme of this book has not been, I fear, entirely resisted.

Of course, I am not so naive as to suggest that one may find in these pages the complete formula for a contented life. Before the conditions to human welfare become equally accessible to all, there are persistent problems in politics, economics, and social relationships which must be solved by intelligent, collective action. These are matters with which the American must preoccupy himself as a citizen. But regardless of the age or the environment in which he lives, the individual cannot escape a residuum of indivisible responsibility for the attainment of his own happiness. Where the conditions to his well-being are contingent, he must act as a citizen; but where they are purely a matter of his own will and initiative, he must bestir himself as an individual.

There is much that he can do to give his leisure hours a creatively significant content. I have emphasized activities and attitudes that seem to me most frequently neglected sources of felicity. Implicit in the various anecdotes relating to the experience of the immigrant, and in all the trivia about bread and wine, is the simple lesson that the home is the appropriate place where man may realize some part of his dignity. Temperance and imagination in the nourishment of the body are homely virtues which may be achieved with ever increasing joy. A sane economy in the administration of domestic affairs should be an attribute of all men regardless of their circumstances. Resourcefulness and self-reliance in providing for the family's immediate needs are ancestral virtues which one should strive to rediscover. The pursuit of these ends will yield a measure of contentment of which no man should deprive himself.

The emphasis which I have placed on food and drink may need some elucidation. The cuisine may be generally regarded as a part of a people's culture. The quality of the fare, the manner in which it is prepared, the time devoted to its ingestion, the conventions of the dinner table: these are intimately related to, and frequently reflect, a people's esthetic development. The Europeans and the Asiatics have developed their traditional cuisine by utilizing in the highest possible degree the resources peculiar to their time and place. Across the centuries and by imperceptible degrees, they have made it an integral part of their culture.

The American, lacking the spur of necessity and engrossed in the exploitation of resources with which no other nation has been blessed in anything like the same degree, has been understandably satisfied to feed on plain meat and potatoes. His curiosity about culinary matters, of relatively recent origin, is an encouraging sign. If he would proceed wisely, however, he must remember that the evolution of a traditional cuisine requires time. His immediate concern should be a willingness to experiment, an insistence upon quality, a purging of his mind of all culinary prejudice, and the development of a humane attitude toward the dinner hour. These, and not a slavish imitation of for-eign recipes and esoteric menus, are the bases upon which a sound American cuisine may be eventually developed.

He must also guard himself against a danger to which he is predisposed by his esthetic naïveté: the tendency to be easily impressed by cults and coteries of foreign descent. The culinary poseurs, foreign and domestic alike, are out to capitalize on American cre-dulity in cultural matters. Their insistence that cook-ing is an art and eating and drinking a ritual, has thrown the dinner hour out of focus and produced needless confusion. There are few Americans, for ex-ample, who can serve a dinner which deviates a little from the native tradition without being somewhat self-conscious about it. And who is certain about when to serve red and when to serve white wine? The proper attitude, of course, is that it doesn't make a damned bit of difference.

I have emphasized bread and wine as ingredients in the good life, for a further reason. As an immigrant, the discovery of abundance has been the most palpa-ble and the most impressive of my discoveries in America. Nothing so much as this fact has brought home to me the spectacular contrast between my old home and my new. I have sought to communicate the personal significance of this fact to my fellow Ameri-cans in the hope that it may awaken them to a more keen realization of their heritage and make them aware of their responsibility in preserving the nation's resources for the children of tomorrow.

As the years pass and I become more and more identified with my new home, this initial discovery remains an important clue to the meaning of America. I have observed, for example, that in his attitude to-ward food the American reveals significant aspects of his character. The endemic waste, the exclusive reliance upon the grocer and the butcher for all his culinary needs, the obliviousness to what grows freely in the environment—do not these reflect his indifference to frugality as a virtue, and his subservience to what I have called the quantitative fallacy? Where the game everywhere played is for high stakes, there is no understandable value in any bend of effort unless its relevance to some large undertaking is immediately perceptible. Frugality in itself, the prudent use of Nature's gifts, is meaningless. In a land that idolizes the Rockefellers and the Fords, the growing of a carrot and a cabbage seems a trifling preoccupation—unless, perhaps, they can be exhibited as the *biggest* carrot and the *biggest* cabbage ever grown anywhere.

There is yet no evidence that the experience of the war years has had the salutary effect for which some of us had hoped. The American still wastes and continues to trample underfoot whatever does not measure up to his gigantic illusions. He does not yet perceive the consequences of having used with reckless imprudence the precious yield of the good earth; he does not realize that the quantitative analysis of value is fundamentally deceptive; nor does he yet see with any clarity that, in his uncritical devotion to big things, he has neglected the trifles which, in their totality, constitute a principal ingredient in human happiness.

I should not be at all hesitant to say that, of the principal ingredients, it is the most important, and that this book may therefore be properly regarded as a continuous emphasis on neglected trifles: the garden, the cellar, the simple pleasures of the dinner hour, a scrupulous husbandry in the home, the quiet joy of modest achievement. These are all phases of what ought to be one of man's central preoccupations

—the attempt to discover within his own domain the felicity he cannot find in the market place.

I am perfectly aware that I am insisting upon old-fashioned virtues, and that there is a touch of agrarian décor in the inducements I am offering my fellows to join me in eccentric anachronisms. And that, of course, is precisely my intention. The best and the wisest of men—oh, certainly there have been exceptions!—have found solace within the garden gate. "God Almighty," said Bacon, "first planted a garden; and, indeed, it is the purest of human pleasures; it is the greatest refreshment to the spirits of man; without which buildings and palaces are but gross handiworks; and a man shall ever see that, when ages grow to civility and elegance, man comes to build stately, sooner than to garden finely; as if gardening were the greater perfection."

The bleak winter months have passed, and the earth is relaxing under the incipient sun. Beneath the kitchen window, the wild violet is in bloom, the azalea, the tulip, and the daffodil are swelling with life. The chicory planted in the fall is sending succulent shoots through the softening crust of ground. The first green onions will soon be ready for the table. Bleached and hidden in the mulch, the dandelion is waiting for the frugal immigrant. The sap is rising in the peach tree and the blush of life is visible in its buds.

Each morning, before I set out for the classroom, I walk leisurely through my diminutive estate. As Charles Lamb, at his home in Edmonton, "watched with interest the progress toward maturity of his Windsor pears and jargonelles," so I delight in the first flowers and survey in anticipated pleasure the tender shoots of leafy delicacies that I shall have with my evening meal.

I know that my butcher, who serves me so well, will

have my favorite cut of meat when I shall call at his shop at the end of the day's work. What will it be? A roast? A steak? Sweetbreads? Lamb kidneys? Whatever the choice, it will be prepared with care and served with the appropriate vegetable from the garden.

Before dinner there will be the customary descent down the cellar stairs, with the infant gourmet at my heels, into the cubicle of Temperance. I will see there a sight familiar enough: shelves stocked with last year's produce from the garden; mushrooms from the meadows and the hills; sea food from the waters of Puget Sound; bottles of red and white wine of various ages; and the cradled oak barrels in which last year's vintage is "breathing through the wood." A sight familiar enough! But always evocative, pleasantly reassuring, and mildly exciting.

It is not an inadequate symbol of the fusion of two cultures. What I have called the cubicle of Temperance reflects the tangible results of the immigrant's thrift, his industry and resourcefulness, his high culinary standards, and his instinct for humane living, when these have found scope in the prodigality of the American environment. Mere trifles? Of course! But they can be transmuted into the indispensable means to a better life.

AFTERWORD

M. F. K. Fisher

Although I have known very few men of letters intimately, excluding my husbands, of course, Angelo Pellegrini is the only one I have ever shared a spit-bucket
with.

Perhaps the nearest I ever came to this was one noon-
time in a heat spell in New York, in about 1944, when I
waited a long time for Somerset Maugham to get up from
his luncheon rendez-vous with a handsome blonde and
then sat as soon as possible on his chair. It was warmer
than the weather, almost hot from his plump old bottom,
and I felt it voluptuously through my whole being, like
fine tea or perhaps a noble Chambertin sat upon and in,
rather than drunk as common mortals would absorb it.

And sharing a bucket at the Pomona County Fair-
grounds with Angelo Pellegrini, in about 1946, was even
headier . . . or perhaps I should say soul-shaking. He
detested me.

It was at the Los Angeles County Fair in Pomona. To
please an old good family friend, Harold Richardson, I
had agreed to be one of his crew in the first serious public
wine-judging south of Sacramento, from whence had
come all our official vinous nods until then. Of course we
were frowned on, by anyone south of Santa Barbara, for
stepping on hallowed tradition, but Harold felt that the
time was right, and he asked a mixed lot to meet with him
at the Fair Grounds "down south." I was the only female

there, and in fact the first of my sex ever to be on a California wine panel, as far as I know.

Of course it was very hot in September, and I dressed for coolness and changed my usual personal habits only by cutting out all soap and toothpaste and lotions and perfumes for two weeks; I did not smoke anyway, but I stopped any tea-coffee-wine-booze for five days before the judging. In other words, I was a Good Girl, a white Anglo-Saxon non-Christian.

The equipment for judging was very primitive then. For one thing, we were supposed to "do" about 180 bottled products in three days. For another, the "judges" were seated two by two at a long table with of course the bottles-on-hand and the sparse glasses in front of each one and then a bucket, a plain old five-gallon bucket, between each pair. No dentist-office neat installations!

The first day we judged white wines. The second we whipped through reds. The third and final day we did fruit wines in the morning and brandies after lunch, and toward the end of that day we swallowed quite a bit, instead of spitting it hopefully toward our partners and fairly deftly into our shared buckets.

I had a hard time spitting in public, at first. I knew I would have to when I accepted Harold's invitation, because I had watched wine men do it nonchalantly in Burgundy and Switzerland. But they were always *men*. I had never seen a woman do it, probably because they never went into the courtyards outside their husbands' wineries when anyone was there. I did not count there as a woman, being a foreigner and by nature invisible anyway. But in Pomona, when I had to spit like a man, facing my companion across the bucket and trying to guess what he thought of the wine we had just let swirl and unfold in our separate mouths, I was at first almost appalled at myself. I was nearing forty, and I had never done such a thing as *spit*, except in a closed private space, and alone.

My partner was Angelo Pellegrini. At least, that was what was marked on our cards and announced in the sheet Harold had sent to each judge.

I admired Angelo very much, and felt awed that I would actually meet him at Harold's little gatherings. I reread THE UNPREJUDICED PALATE, and felt more strongly than ever that it was the first true statement I had yet read about living as it can and should be in the western coastal America that I love. It did not occur to me that I would have to *spit* in front of this Pan-like man. And for a while it looked as if I wouldn't.

I sat alone at my slot and pretended to taste a few white wines, and watched how my neighbors acted, and even learned how to eject the juices without dribbling, before Harold hurried in from his office with a short dark furious man fuming alongside. Introductions were impossible as Harold's replacement put us through our paces and we gradually got into our own rhythms of tasting, marking, moving along through the rows of unmarked bottles. Beside me Angelo inhaled and swirled and swished noisily, and spat contemptuously almost everywhere but into our bucket, our private shared spittoon.

He was plainly in a gigantic rage.

And at noon, after one of the most miserable mornings of my life, Harold told me that Angelo had roared into his office a few minutes before the judging started and had said that he would never consent to have a woman present at a wine-tasting, much less sit next to *him*. He swore in two or three languages and was noisy in every possible way. He was, in other words, an insulted Italian, than which . . .

Harold, in his own more decorous way, was furious at having his actions called whatever Angelo called them, and finally he assumed all his legal sternness and said *put up or shut up*, and Angelo agreed to sit by me for one day.

But after lunch he stormed into Harold's office again

and said that he could not go on. He was leaving for Seattle *this afternoon.*

Harold, by now smooth and silky and in general the
successful criminal lawyer trying his most important
case, had no need to counter-question his client to discover that not only was the person appointed as his fellow
wine judge a female, but that she *smelled.* She smelled of
PERFUME. She was plainly unfit to sit next to a highly
qualified and respected wine man-author-*bon viveur*, a
true American but also a living example of good Italian
sensitivity and general machismo. "She must go," he
said. "Or . . . *I* go. She stinks."

Of course all these stormings were a painful interrup-
tion to Harold's plans to direct and cosset and teach and
in general bend his first selected jury to his enological
will. It was his show. He was supposed to be out there
leading his flock, not closeted with a wild-eyed sputter-
ing Italian professor. It was probably self-survival that got
him to seat Angelo beside me again, still unintroduced
and openly sneering, but able to function as a wine *judge.*
(He still spat before I did, and in several directions, and
never looked at me or spoke.)

After work that night, Harold took me to dinner and
told me, as soft-voiced and gentle as always, that Angelo
Pellegrini, the man I so admired for his vital literary
style, said I smelled. "To me, you do not," Harold added
firmly, and I told him of my ascetic preparations for his
unprecedented panel of wine judges, and he smiled ap-
proval in his usual avuncular-paternal manner, and said
something like "Carry on!" We finished our unusually
dull meal, saltless-sauceless-wineless for our palates' pu-
rity and next day's scheduled REDS, and parted without
visible tears.

It was a bad day, but at least Angelo was there the whole
time. He never looked at me or spoke, but his spitting was
spotless. Whenever Harold picked up our scorecards he

smiled a little, because we seemed to be marking the same things about the same bottles. . . .

The next day was the last, thank God. I had never lived through such a miserable experience. My female honor felt bruised by the dark unsmiling man sitting with such obvious impatience and distaste beside me, sharing the same horrid bucket for our public rinsings, sucking in his breath whenever I had to lean toward him so that I would not pollute his pristine taste buds with my stench. I prayed for patience to get through the fruit wines, through the raw brandies, and away.

When we went into the plain bleak room, the glasses and first bottles and buckets were set out, and we placed ourselves, but Harold and Angelo were not there. In about ten minutes they hurried out and almost ran toward me, so that I stood up anxiously: was it bad news about my little girls, my ailing mother?

Angelo, flashing a beautiful boyish giddying smile, bowed low over my hand, and kissed it passionately. Harold almost danced around us. Probably all the other judges, middle-aged respected medicos and tycoons and physicists, looked on with bemused patience, ignorant of our little drama, as Angelo begged me to forgive him for his cruel actions and Harold explained patchily but almost as passionately that Angelo's motel soap smelled, and therefore he smelled, and especially his hands smelled. *I did not.*

The rest is obvious. Years fell from my shoulders, and I was young, beautiful, desirable. Angelo was alive beside me, as only a healthy Italian can be. We spat in unison into the suddenly attractive puddle of fruit juice and water we shared, and a newspaper paparazzo from Los Angeles shot our jets meeting in midair just above the bucket. And halfway through the long last afternoon tasting of brandies we all began to *swallow*, and ignored most of the other rules, so that before we all parted after a fine meal of heavily spiced delicacies and plenty of our best bottles from the first two days, I was *carissima* forever, to the Pan of the Pacific Coast, Angelo Pellegrini.

I still am, with the full consent of his wife, and the tacit agreement of scores of other fellow females in every direction from Seattle. Now and then Angelo remembers me, and sends me a clipping of something he has written, or a picture of his prize pumpkin, or a blurred snapshot of a new grandchild, all askew but eminently handsome and healthy because they came from Angelo Pellegrini: from him, the great god Pan of this Western world.

1984

Titles available from
THE COOK'S CLASSIC LIBRARY

Lyons & Burford, Publishers
31 West 21 Street · New York, New York 10010
(tel) 212/620-9580 · (fax) 212/929-1836